AJ

dinosaurs

a *flowmotion*™ title

dinosaurs

dr. emily rayfield

Sterling Publishing Co., Inc.
New York

Created and conceived by
Axis Publishing Limited
8c Accommodation Road
London NW11 8ED
www.axispublishing.co.uk

Creative Director: Siân Keogh
Managing Editor: Brian Burns
Project Designer: Axis Design Editions
Project Editor: Conor Kilgallon
Production Controller: Juliet Brown

Illustrations: Chris Taylor 1, 10, 11, 14, 16, 20, 28–29,
30–31, 36–37, 40–41, 42–43, 66–67, 70–71, 74–75, 76–77,
86–87, 88–89; Thumbprint Animation 3, 5, 6, 12, 17, 18,
19, 24, 46–47, 48–49, 50–51, 54–55, 56–57, 58–59, 60–61,
62–63, 64–65, 68–69, 72–73, 78–79, 80–81, 82–83, 84–85,
90–91.

Library of Congress Cataloging-in-Publication Data
Available

10 9 8 7 6 5 4 3 2 1

Published in 2003 by Sterling Publishing Co., Inc.
387 Park Avenue South, New York, NY 10016
Text and images © Axis Publishing Limited 2003
Distributed in Canada by Sterling Publishing
C/o Canadian Manda Group,
One Atlantic Avenue, Suite 105
Toronto, Ontario, Canada, M6K 3E7

ISBN 0–8069–9371–5

Printed by Star Standard (Pte) Limited

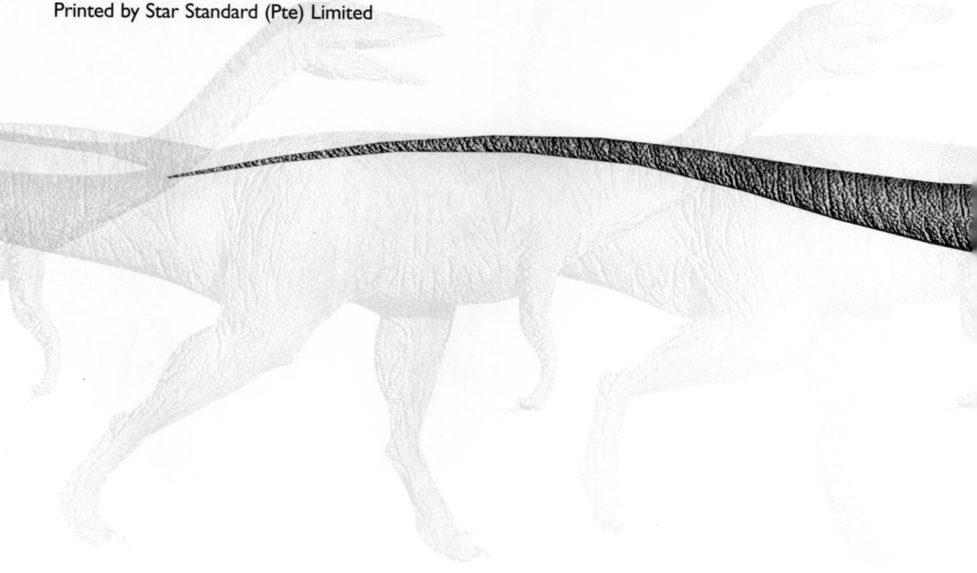

a *flow**motion***™ title

dinosaurs

contents

introduction

In many ways, you are built just like a dinosaur. You have arms, legs, wrists, ankles, elbows, and knees, as did the dinosaurs. You have shoulders, hips, calves, and thighs, as did the dinosaurs. Dinosaurs had noses, ears, and eyes similar to yours, to smell, hear, and see the world. They had a bony skeleton, and muscles, ligaments, and tendons to generate movement, in the same way as they do in your own body.

The reason why we are alike in this way is that dinosaurs and humans are distantly related to each other. Many hundreds of millions of years ago, one branch of the ancient family of animals became more like mammals (humans are a type of mammal), and long after the dinosaurs became extinct, modern humans appeared.

The dawn of the dinosaurs, or "terrible lizards," around 230 million years ago created a breed of animals never seen before on Planet Earth.

Dinosaurs were well adapted for living in new ways by being able to run fast, or by being exceedingly large or exceptionally ferocious. In this book we will examine the most important dinosaurs, what they looked like, when and how they lived, and how they moved.

when did the dinosaurs live?

Dinosaurs ruled the Earth during an era of time known as the "Mesozoic." The Mesozoic is divided into three time periods, called the Triassic, Jurassic, and Cretaceous. The Triassic period began around 245 million years ago (MYA), yet dinosaurs did not appear until 15 million years later. The first

Herrerasaurus is one of the earliest known dinosaurs. It lived in South America about 230 million years ago.

dinosaurs were rare animals, found scattered throughout what is now Argentina in South America around 230 MYA.

From these humble beginnings dinosaurs spread quickly into other continents so that by the start of the Jurassic period nearly 30 million years later, they could be found all over the world. The Jurassic period stretched from 201 to 144 MYA and was followed by the Cretaceous period from 144 to 65 MYA.

Toward the end of the Cretaceous period, the Earth became colder and drier; then a huge asteroid from space crashed into the Earth near the coast of Mexico. The asteroid destroyed all life in the area and choked the atmosphere with a large cloud of dust and debris. Around 65 MYA the dinosaurs became extinct, possibly finally killed off by the damage done by the asteroid. All was not lost, however, as a small, new group of dinosaurs had by this time given rise to the ancestors of modern-day birds. In some ways, we can think of dinosaurs still living on today in the bodies of sparrows, pigeons, and all other birds.

how did dinosaurs live?

Some dinosaurs grew up to 147ft (46m) long, 48ft (15m) tall and weighed 100 tons. However, not all dinosaurs were so large; in fact, some were very small, the size of a chicken in some cases. "Herbivorous" dinosaurs only ate plants while bloodthirsty types known as "carnivores" ate only meat. A few dinosaurs ate both meat and plants and were known as "omnivores." "Bipedal" dinosaurs walked on two legs, while "quadrupedal" dinosaurs walked on all fours. Certain dinosaurs could choose to walk on either two or four legs. Some dinosaurs could probably swim, although no dinosaur lived in the water.

It must also be remembered that not all animals at this time were dinosaurs. Creatures such as the plesiosaur (which looked like the accepted image of the legendary Loch Ness monster) and the dolphin-like ichthyosaurs lived in water during the Mesozoic, yet were not dinosaurs.

WHAT IS EVOLUTION?

All organisms arise by the process of evolution. Evolution is the development of new types of animals or plants from other animals and plants that already exist. When these animals and plants reproduce, genes that were once hidden may be uncovered, or accidental changes to genes may occur. Sometimes, these changes give offspring an advantage over other members of its own species. These advantages are then passed onto the following generations, which may develop further advantages. When a group of organisms becomes genetically very different to its ancestors, it is called a new "species."

ancestor chart—cladogram

A cladogram is a type of family tree that shows how a group of animals evolved from a common ancestor. Start at the bottom left at "Dinosauria" and work your way along the branches to see who is related to whom. All the major dinosaur groups are in capitals and the names of the dinosaurs themselves come at the end of each branch. The names in bold refer to dinosaurs featured in this book.

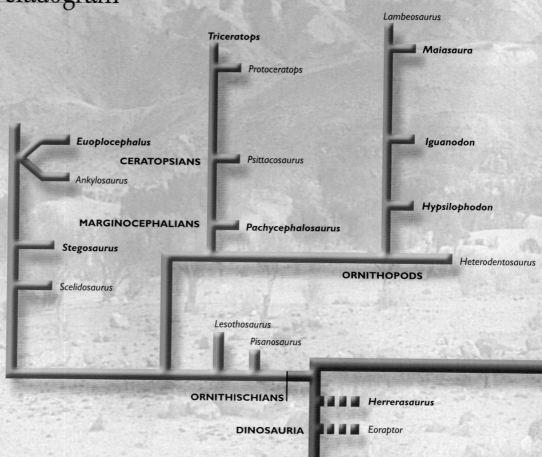

Lambeosaurus

Triceratops

Maiasaura

Protoceratops

Euoplocephalus

CERATOPSIANS

Iguanodon

Ankylosaurus

Psittacosaurus

MARGINOCEPHALIANS

Hypsilophodon

Pachycephalosaurus

Stegosaurus

THYREOPHORANS

Heterodentosaurus

Scelidosaurus

ORNITHOPODS

Lesothosaurus

Pisanosaurus

ORNITHISCHIANS

Herrerasaurus

DINOSAURIA

Eoraptor

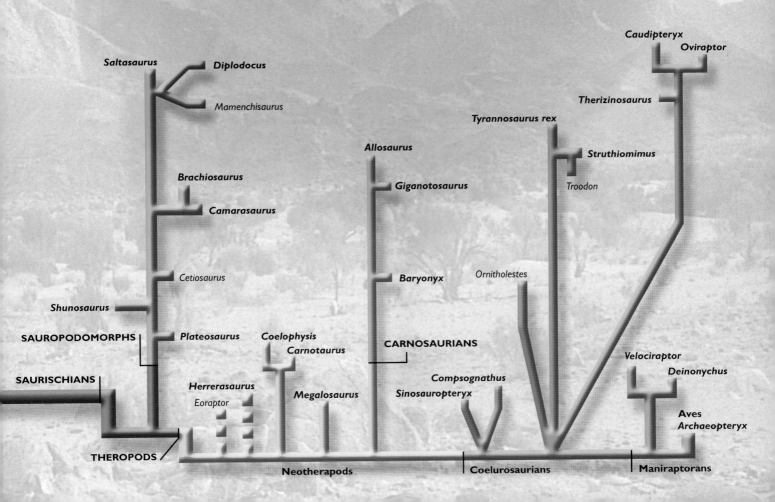

Saltasaurus

Diplodocus

Mamenchisaurus

Caudipteryx

Oviraptor

Therizinosaurus

Tyrannosaurus rex

Struthiomimus

Allosaurus

Troodon

Brachiosaurus

Giganotosaurus

Camarasaurus

Cetiosaurus

Baryonyx

Ornitholestes

Shunosaurus

SAUROPODOMORPHS

Plateosaurus

Coelophysis

Carnotaurus

CARNOSAURIANS

Velociraptor

Deinonychus

SAURISCHIANS

Herrerasaurus

Eoraptor

Megalosaurus

Compsognathus

Sinosauropteryx

Aves
Archaeopteryx

THEROPODS

Neotherapods

Coelurosaurians

Maniraptorans

dinosaur groups—hips and beak tips

Dinosaurs are generally divided into two major groups, the "saurischians" and the "ornithischians," depending on the shape of the hips and a small bone in the skull.

Hips are made up of three different bones: the ilium, the ischium, and the pubis. In all dinosaurs the ilium is fused (fixed) to the backbone, and the ischium points backward and downward from the ilium. In the saurischians, the third bone, the pubis, points forward and downward. The saurischians are sometimes called "lizard-hipped," as their arrangement of bones can still be seen in modern crocodiles and other extinct relatives of dinosaurs.

In the ornithischians, however, the pubis changed direction and faced backward and downward. Ornithischians are sometimes called "bird-hipped" as birds also have a backward-pointing pubis. This term is confusing, however, as ornithischians are not actually the ancestors of birds. Some saurischian dinosaurs developed backward-facing pubis bones as well, so grouping dinosaurs together can sometimes be confusing. Also, all

Below: *Diplodocus* was a type of saurischian dinosaur. Saurischians were were often distinguished by a forward-pointing pubis bone in their hips.

Opposite: *Triceratops* was a type of ornithischian dinosaur, with a backward-pointing pubis bone in its hip.

ornithischian dinosaurs have a small bone called the "predentary" at the tip of their lower jaw. The predentary forms the lower part of a small beak and is not found in saurischian dinosaurs.

saurischians—the large versus the ferocious

Saurischians are divided into two main groups, the "sauropodomorphs" and the "theropods." All saurischians originally had an long second finger and an "opposable thumb," like we have, so they could grasp greenery or prey between finger and thumb.

Sauropodomorphs divide into prosauropods and sauropods. Prosauropods were fairly large, plant-eating dinosaurs with long necks and tails, capable of walking on two or four legs. Sauropods were large, herbivorous, four-legged animals with extremely long necks and tails. *Diplodocus*, *Brachiosaurus*, and *Apatosaurus* were all sauropod dinosaurs. Theropods were generally, though not always, meat eaters. *Tyrannosaurus rex*, *Velociraptor*, and *Allosaurus* were all famous theropod dinosaurs. We will discover later in the book how a particular group of theropod dinosaurs gave rise to birds.

ornithischians

Ornithischians fall into three main groups. The first group, the "thyreophorans," walked on all fours and had armor plating on their bodies. *Stegosaurus* and *Ankylosaurus* are two well-known thyreophorans. The second group, the "ornithopods," walked on either two legs or a combination of two and four legs. They include the duck-billed dinosaurs and *Iguanodon*. The group Marginocephalia includes pachycephalosaurs—bipedal animals with large domed heads—and ceratopsians, originally bipedal animals that later came down onto all fours to become quadrupeds. The horned dinosaurs *Triceratops* and *Styracosaurus* are well-known ceratopsians.

All ornithischian dinosaurs were herbivores. Plants are difficult to eat and require lots of chewing or stomach-based fermentation to release their nutrients. Some researchers have suggested that ornithischians moved their pubis backward in order make space for a large plant-fermenting gut.

how dinosaurs moved

general requirements

All animals must be able to do certain things to be able to move, and dinosaurs were no exception. They must be able to support their body weight while staying stable and not fall over, even when quickly changing direction. They must use the energy they get from food to get their bodies moving and keep them moving.

dinosaur success

Despite huge differences in their size, shape, and diet, all dinosaurs evolved from a fast-moving, bipedal ancestor. Different groups of dinosaurs went on to modify their skeletons in different ways to suit their chosen lifestyle. One of the reasons that dinosaurs survived for millions of years is that their legs and bodies were very well-suited for moving about on land.

sprawling

Modern lizards and crocodiles have a "sprawling posture." These animals hold their limbs out to the sides of their bodies, much like a human doing a push-up. The upper bones

Like all dinosaurs, *Iguanodon* had an "upright posture" with its limbs and feet tucked beneath its body, rather than held out to the sides.

in the forelimb (the humerus) and the hindlimb (the femur) are held horizontally to the body, while the lower limb bones (called the radius and ulna in the forelimb and the tibia and fibula in the hindlimb) are held vertically. If you have ever seen a crocodile or a lizard move, you will also know that the backbone and tail swing from side to side as they move. This swinging motion helps move their feet and hands forward to increase the length of every step. The elbows, knees, wrists, and ankles also twist to help keep the feet and hands planted flat on the ground.

As "sprawlers" keep their bodies close to the ground with their feet placed widely apart, they are very stable and difficult to knock over. As anyone who performs push-ups knows, it is very difficult to support your weight on bent arms in this way. This means that sprawlers tend not to be large, heavy animals.

upright success
The very distant ancestors of dinosaurs were sprawlers, but dinosaur limbs were positioned differently. Dinosaurs tucked their limbs directly beneath their bodies in what is known as "upright posture." All the limb bones were held roughly vertical, and the feet were kept underneath the body rather than placed widely apart.

Dinosaurs tended to keep their backbones more rigid in order to prevent the side-to-side swinging seen in sprawlers. Moving the limbs became much more important than moving the backbone. The hips were also firmly fused to the backbone, which helped them to cope with the pressure put on the bones by movement. Rather than twisting, dinosaur limb joints could only move in a forward and backward direction like a hinge, similar to our own knees. So rather than looking like lizard arms and legs, dinosaur limbs moved more like mammal limbs, such as those of a dog.

By holding the limbs underneath the body, rather than out to the side, the legs can support a greater body weight (we have seen how difficult push-ups are). Holding the limb bones vertically also increases the length of each step (the stride). Like birds and some mammals, dinosaurs developed a special hinge bone enabling them to walk on their fingers and toes. This is known as "digitigrade" posture. Digitigrade walking increases the length of the legs and therefore increases stride length.

Animals with upright limbs are also able to change direction better and more quickly than sprawlers, although upright posture is less stable than sprawling, as the feet are placed closer together and most of the body weight is held further from the ground.

Dinosaurs tended to have long tails to balance the weight of the head and neck and to keep the body steady during walking and running.

muscles

In dinosaurs, powerful muscles ran from the hips and tail to the legs, and from the shoulders to the arms. When the dinosaur placed its hands and feet on the ground, these muscles pulled the legs and arms backwards, pushing the body forward over the legs.

In nearly all dinosaurs, the most powerful leg muscle was the "caudofemoralis." This muscle ran from the tail to near the top of the thigh bone and helped pull the leg backward.

Other muscles were designed specially for lifting the leg and pulling it forward, or placing the leg on the ground to begin a stride. Further muscles helped bend and straighten the knees, elbows, and other joints.

Further muscles helped to keep the animal upright—especially important for bipedal dinosaurs. We shall see later how changes to the hip, limb, and tail bones helped dinosaurs alter how these muscles worked and how this affected the way they moved.

Dinosaurs such as *Giganotosaurus* (shown here) moved by contracting powerful muscles running from the hips and tail to the legs.

gait

If you are walking slowly and want to speed up, you start to move your legs faster and increase the length of your steps. Eventually, you break into a slow run. Walking and running are known as different types of "gaits," or sequences of leg movements. During walking, each foot spends more than half of its total stride on the ground. During running, each foot spends less than half the stride in contact with the ground.

At high speed, animals may run or use other gaits such as trotting, bounding, or galloping, like a horse. As we will see later in this book, some dinosaurs could run, while others could only manage a fast walk.

size and speed

A human child needs to run to keep up with a walking adult. This is because as animals get bigger, they can take longer (and fewer strides) than smaller animals. Larger animals use up more total energy to move, but save some energy as they take fewer strides than smaller animals. Many dinosaurs were very large and may have taken advantage of this fact. Large dinosaurs could have roamed large areas for food, drink, shelter, and mating. Their large size meant that once they were adults, they were also less likely to be attacked by smaller predatory dinosaurs.

Also, large dinosaurs had a very large body volume, meaning that lots of heat could be contained within the body. They did not cool down very quickly and were able to keep a fairly stable body temperature, even in the cold of night (see hot- and cold-blooded box on p. 17).

Brachiosaurus could not run. However, it was so large and its stride was so long that smaller animals had to run just to keep up.

HOW FAST CAN YOU RUN?

You can calculate your own speed using a stopwatch and some measuring tape. Run for 10 seconds, and then measure how far you have managed to run. Speed can be measured in feet or meters per second. If you ran 150ft (45m) in 10 seconds, this means you were running at an average speed of 15ft (4.5m) per second (150 divided by 10). How does this compare to dinosaur speeds? Do you think you could outrun a *T.rex*?

measuring up

As we have seen, growing large has its advantages, but as an animal increases in size, the sheer strength of the bones it needs and the amount of force the muscles must produce to move the animal become a real problem. To prevent growing huge, heavy bones and muscles, large animals must modify the shape of their skeleton and alter their way of life.

To avoid jolting the skeleton, large animals tend not to run or gallop. During walking, the limbs tend not to move far in order to guard against over-stretching bones and muscles. Large animals often position their limbs as upright as possible to avoid bending bones.

Sauropod dinosaurs approached the size limit for land animals. In water, weight problems are greatly reduced, as water actually helps buoy the skeleton. Animals such as modern blue whales can grow to much greater sizes than the land-based dinosaurs ever could.

Shunosaurus and other sauropods modified their limbs and gait to carry their large, heavy bodies.

energy conservation

Large animals use lots of energy when they move, so any way of conserving energy is very welcome. Choice of gait is important, as walking quickly, for example, can use less energy than running slowly at the same speed. Gravity also helps direct the swinging limb toward the ground and tip the body forward over the leg, like the pendulum of a large clock.

The tendons are another important energy store. Tendons are sheets or ropes of elastic fibers that connect muscles to bone. Long tendons run down the legs of many animals (you may be able to feel them behind your knee). As the foot is placed on the ground, the tendon is stretched, storing energy just like a giant elastic band. When the foot is taken off the ground, energy is released from the tendon and the leg springs backward and upward. Tendons are important energy stores in large animals such as horses and camels and probably were in dinosaurs as well.

Ligaments connect bones to other bones. They are less elastic than tendons, but ligaments can act as important energy stores as well, for example in the human foot while walking. Sometimes muscles, tendons, and ligaments all combine to store energy during movement.

Theropod dinosaurs and birds, including *Archaeopteryx*, have hollow bones to lighten their skeletons.

Some animals, such as elephants, have pads of fatty tissue supporting their heels to cushion the heavy impact of their feet when they hit the ground. Some dinosaurs, especially sauropods, probably had the same pads.

By reducing the weight of the body, less energy is needed to carry it around. Bone is quite heavy, so making bones thinner helps save energy. It is important, however, that although bones are light, they must also be strong enough not to break when moving quickly: there is a trade-off between strength and lightness.

Bones may be fused together to increase strength, and digits and toes lost or reduced in size to keep weight down. The body makes sure that bone is produced only where necessary, and excess bone, which is heavy to carry, is removed.

Theropod dinosaurs evolved hollow limb bones, like the bones of mammals and birds. Hollow bones are lighter than solid ones and are actually less likely to bend than solid bones weighing the same amount. All these adaptations ensured that dinosaur movement was as fast and efficient as possible.

HOT- OR COLD-BLOODED DINOSAURS?

Hot-blooded, or "endothermic," animals, such as humans, other mammals, and birds, produce their own body heat to keep warm. Food and oxygen are burned in the body to produce energy and heat to keep muscles and other bodily processes working well. Endothermic animals require lots of food, water, and oxygen to do this, but can keep moving for long periods of time.

Cold-blooded, or "ectothermic" animals, such as snakes and lizards, gain most of their body heat by basking in the sun. Ectotherms require less food, water, and oxygen. They are capable of short bursts of speed, but cannot keep moving fast over long periods of time. Scientists do not know whether dinosaurs were ecto- or endothermic. With their limbs held beneath their bodies, dinosaurs were built for an active lifestyle, suggesting they could produce their own body heat. Also, dinosaur babies could grow quickly (as can baby mammals and birds), and the structure of dinosaur bone is similar to that of endothermic mammals.

As we have seen, large dinosaurs lost heat very slowly. Some smaller dinosaurs were clothed in feathers or feather-like bristles that may have helped conserve body heat. Looking at all the evidence, it seems likely that dinosaurs were endotherms, or at least in-between. This means that they did not depend on the sun to warm their muscles in order to move fast over a long period.

how do we know how dinosaurs moved?

Dinosaurs were once living, breathing creatures, yet all that remains of their existence are bones, teeth, fossilized droppings, and footprints. How can we know how they stood, walked, and ran? How do we know how fast they were or how they lived? How can we write books like this? The following section explains how the scientists who study prehistory—palaeontologists—bring dinosaurs back to life, and, importantly, how confident they are in their conclusions.

bones, joints, and muscles

We have already discovered the many bones that make up a dinosaur arm or leg. The point where a major limb bone joins another is called a "joint." Knees, elbows, ankles, and wrists are all joints. Often, the surfaces of the bones that meet at the joint have unusual hollows, bumps, or lumps that only allow limbs to move in a certain direction. In well-preserved fossils, palaeontologists can examine these lumps and bumps to discover how limb bones fitted and moved together.

In a living animal, a layer known as cartilage covers the joint surface to protect it, and ligaments, muscles, and tendons also hold the bones in position. Small roughened areas, ridges, or dimples on the surface of dinosaur bones may tell us where ligaments, muscles, and tendons were fixed to bone in real life, but these ligaments, muscles, and tendons decompose after death much quicker than bone and so are generally not fossilized.

Palaeontologists can sometimes reconstruct muscles to give a better idea of how a leg or arm moved. Often the muscles of living relatives of dinosaurs, such as crocodiles and birds, are examined to provide clues as to how dinosaur muscles were arranged. The limb muscles of most dinosaurs are similar to crocodile legs muscles, with modifications for upright posture. Changes in the shape of the skeleton are often linked to changes in muscle size, shape, and direction of pull. Palaeontologists use this information to work out how these muscle changes altered dinosaur locomotion.

Lumps and bumps on the bones of dinosaurs such as *Megalosaurus* tell us how their limbs fitted together and how their bones moved against each other.

With its long legs and ability to run fast, *Struthiomimus* is an example of a cursorial dinosaur.

leg shape

Animals that can run fast for long periods of time or over long distances are known as "cursors," and their behavior is called "cursorial." Some scientists have noticed that mammals that have the ability to run fast all have similar-shaped legs. The lower limb bones tend to be longer than the upper limb bones. Also, the long bones of the hands and feet tend to be elongated. This increases stride length.

Bones may be quite thin and when muscles are attached to a limb close to the joint of two bones, using the muscle makes the limb move quickly rather than with great strength. This means that a cursorial animal is able to accelerate to its maximum speed very quickly.

Cursors have the advantage of being able to search large areas quickly for food, drink, and mates, and migrate to other areas as the seasons change. Large, heavy animals can only increase speed slowly while smaller, lighter animals can change speed or direction quickly. Cursors may use speed to catch prey or escape from predators. Cursors can often track or chase prey over large areas before capture. African hunting dogs, ostriches, and horses are all modern cursors.

pondering animals

Scientists also discovered that very large, slow-moving mammals all had similar-shaped legs. In these heavy animals, the upper limb bones, nearest the hip and shoulder, tend to be longer than the lower limb bones, the opposite of what we find in cursors. Pondering animals' limb bones are thicker than cursors' bones, their feet tend to be broad and supportive and leg muscles are adapted for producing force rather than speed. These types of animals are known as "graviportal," meaning "heavy to carry." An elephant is a good example of a graviportal animal.

Careful measurement of dinosaur limb bones has shown that we can find out about the behavior of dinosaurs by looking at the size and shape of their skeletons. This research has shown that the ancestors of all dinosaurs were small, cursorial creatures who evolved into a large variety of weights, body shapes, and sizes.

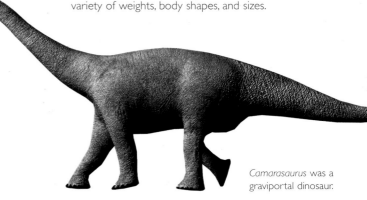

Camarasaurus was a graviportal dinosaur.

footprints

Sometimes palaeontologists find fossilized dinosaur footprints. Footprints and trackways (a series of footprints made by the same animal) provide important clues about dinosaur behavior. Firstly, footprints confirm dinosaurs walked with their legs under their bodies, rather than sprawled out to the side. They also tell us how many toes the dinosaur had, which toes supported most of the weight, whether it walked on two or four legs, and if cushioning foot pads supported the feet.

Some footprints appear to show juvenile bipeds scampering around on all fours, or dinosaurs wading through water and swimming with just the tips of their toes touching the bottom of a lake or shallow sea. Other tracks appear to show herbivorous dinosaurs being followed or chased by predatory meat eaters, although it is impossible to say for certain whether this was the case.

Unless the dinosaur lies dead and fossilized at the end of the trackway, it is very difficult, although not impossible,

Palaeontologists disagree over how fast T.rex could move. Some think it may not have run at all, but no-one can be entirely sure, since no T.rex trackways have yet been found.

to work out which animal a footprint belongs to. Theropods leave three-toed imprints with claw marks at the ends of each toe. Birds also leave three-toed footprints, though the shape of their footprint is different. A large theropod print found in Late Cretaceous rock in New Mexico in the United States is nearly 3ft (1m) long. The only animal we know of large enough to make this print is *Tyrannosaurus rex*. Ornithopods leave broader, three-toed footprints with blunt hoof marks rather than claw marks. Other ornithischians have variable numbers of fingers and toes. Sauropods leave large plate-like hindfoot imprints and smaller semicircular hand prints. The foot pad increases the size of the hind print, which can reach nearly 3ft (1m) in diameter.

calculating speed

Palaeontologists measure dinosaur stride length from lots of footprints found together in the same place. This tells us how far the dinosaur has travelled per stride. We need to know dinosaur leg length and how much time it took the dinosaur to make each stride in order to calculate speed. Legs are roughly four times longer than feet, so leg length can be estimated from footprints.

We cannot measure time by simply looking at the fossils, but luckily, studies on mammals and birds have shown that leg length and stride length are related to speed. As dinosaurs walked like birds and mammals, palaeontologists can use this relationship to calculate dinosaur speeds from their trackways.

It is important to realise that footprints may not record maximum dinosaur speeds, especially since trackways are usually preserved on sticky or slippery surfaces such as wet clay or sand where dinosaurs would have needed to walk slowly and carefully.

strength estimates

Calculations used in engineering have been applied to dinosaurs to find out how strong their bones were. When walking, each foot spends some time on the ground where it takes its turn in supporting the weight of the body. When running, each foot spends only a small amount of time on the ground. Experiments using sensors have shown that runners support forces up to $3^{1}/_{2}$ times their body weight with each foot.

Some dinosaurs were very heavy, and running would have placed large stresses on their limb bones. Working out how strong bones were allows scientists to see if a dinosaur's limbs could have supported up to $3^{1}/_{2}$ times its body weight. These calculations have enabled palaeontologists to estimate whether they could run or not.

muscles

Recently, some scientists have investigated how much muscle a land animal would need to be able to run fast. These researchers used their findings to work out that an adult *T.rex* could not run very fast at all, perhaps between 10–25mph (16–40km/h) *T.rex* may even have been restricted to a fast walk, but this is very new research.

who lived where?

The numbers below relate to the large map of the Earth opposite and show which dinosaurs have been found where. However, the Earth did not always look the way it does today. The continents have shifted dramatically, shown by the small inset maps on the right.

1 WESTERN STATES, USA
DIPLODOCUS, BRACHIOSAURUS, CAMARASAURUS, STEGOSAURUS, MAIASAURA, T.REX, DEINONYCHUS, EUOPLOCEPHALUS

2 ALBERTA, CANADA
TRICERATOPS, PACHYCEPHALOSAURUS, STRUTHIOMIMUS

3 ARIZONA AND NEW MEXICO, USA
COELOPHYSIS

4 ENGLAND
IGUANODON, HYPSILOPHODON, MEGALOSAURUS, BARYONYX

5 GERMANY
COMPSOGNATHUS, ARCHAEOPTERYX, PLATEOSAURUS

6 MONGOLIA
VELOCIRAPTOR, OVIRAPTOR, THERIZINOSAURUS

7 CHINA
SINOSAUROPTERYX, SHUNOSAURUS, CAUDIPTERYX

8 TANZANIA
BRACHIOSAURUS

9 ARGENTINA
SALTASAURUS, HERRERASAURUS, CARNOTAURUS, GIGANOTOSAURUS

PANGAEA

LATE TRIASSIC

LAURASIA

GONDWANALAND

LATE JURASSIC

LATE CRETACEOUS

NORTH AMERICA

SOUTH AMERICA

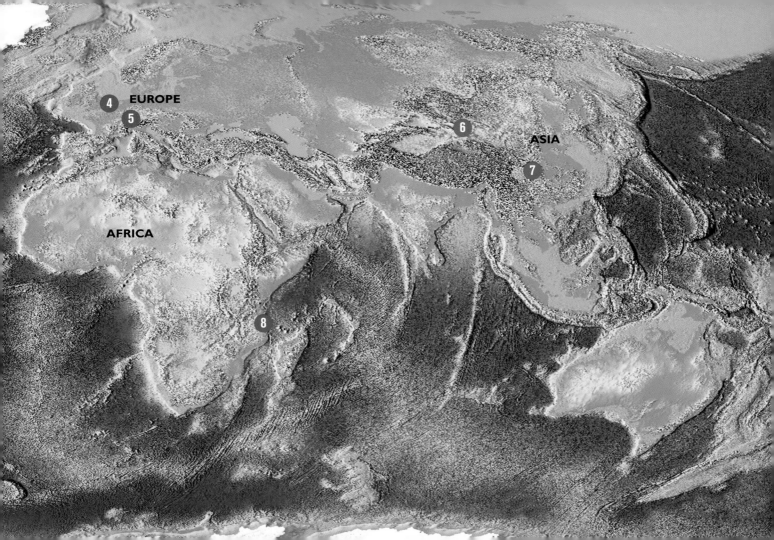

EUROPE

ASIA

AFRICA

4

5

6

7

8

who lived when?

Not all dinosaurs lived at the same time. *T.rex* would never have met *Allosaurus*. Even though the animals lived in the same area, *Allosaurus* existed about 80 million years before *T.rex*. Some dinosaurs, such as *Deinonychus* and *Giganotosaurus*, lived at the same time yet never met, as they inhabited different continents separated by large, open seas. The next section examines which types of dinosaurs lived together and what the climate and environment was like at the time.

There is not enough space in this book to cover all known dinosaurs, and even if this were possible, some dinosaurs are known from only a few pieces of bone—not enough to make useful predictions about their locomotion. When reading the main part of the book, it is important to remember that just because dinosaurs share the same type of locomotion, it does not mean they are closely related.

MILLION YEARS AGO	ERA	PERIOD
0	cenozoic	QUATERNARY
	TERTIARY	NEOGENE
65		PALEOGENE
	mesozoic	CRETACEOUS
144		JURASSIC
206		TRIASSIC
250		PERMIAN
290	paleozoic	CARBONIFEROUS
360		DEVONIAN
410		SILURIAN
440		ORDOVICIAN
510		CAMBRIAN
570		precambrian

PACHYCEPHALOSAURUS

THERIZINOSAURUS

MAIASAURA

OVIRAPTOR

SALTASAURUS

T. REX

VELOCIRAPTOR

EUOPLOCEPHALUS

STRUTHIOMIMUS

TRICERATOPS

LATE

DEINONYCHUS

CARNOTAURUS

GIGANOTOSAURUS

MID

HYPSILOPHODON

SINOSAUROPTERYX

CAUDIPTERYX

BARYONYX

IGUANODON

EARLY

CAMARASAURUS

ARCHAEOPTERYX

DIPLODOCUS

BRACHIOSAURUS

COMPSOGNATHUS

STEGOSAURUS

LATE

MEGALOSAURUS

SHUNOSAURUS

MID

EARLY

HERRERASAURUS

PLATEOSAURUS

COELOPHYSIS

LATE

65
70
75
80
85
90
95
100
105
110
115
120
125
130
135
140
145
150
155
160
165
170
175
180
185
190
195
200
205
210
215
220
225
230
235
240
245

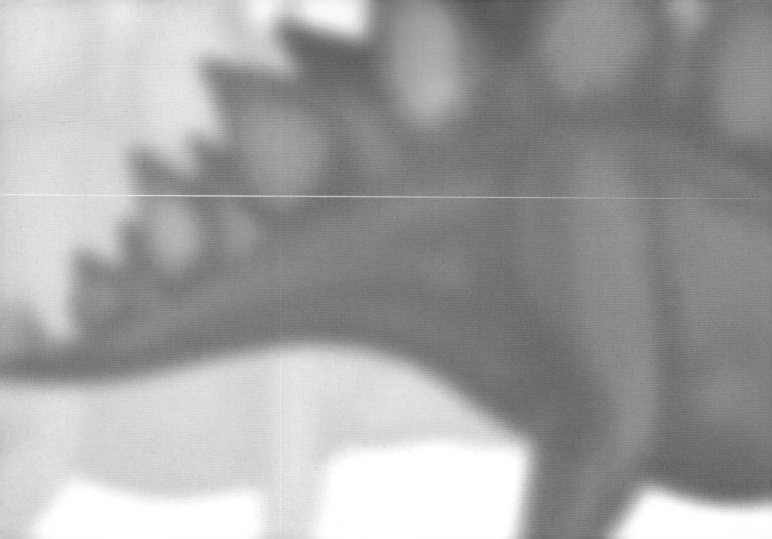

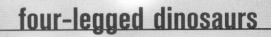

four-legged dinosaurs

shunosaurus

Shunosaurus (Shu lizard) was an early sauropod from the Middle Jurassic of China. All sauropods were large, herbivorous four-legged animals that existed from the Late Triassic until the Late Cretaceous. Along with the prosauropods, they belong to a group called sauropodomorphs. Sauropodomorphs are saurischian dinosaurs—animals with a forward-pointing pubis bone.

● Sauropods evolved from bipedal ancestors that increased the length of their forelimbs until they touched the ground to help support their own weight. In *Shunosaurus*, the upper arm bone was still only two-thirds of the length of the thigh bone (femur).

● At around 32ft (10m) long, *Shunosaurus* was a small sauropod compared to later giants such as *Brachiosaurus* (see pp. 34–35), but it had already shifted its arms and legs underneath its body to act as strong, supportive pillars.

● *Shunosaurus* had a long neck and tail, a small head, and a short, deep body. Sometimes the last few tail bones were fused together to make a bony club. Strong muscles at the base of the tail helped swing the club from side to side to scare away predators.

● All sauropods probably used a "symmetrical gait," meaning the left arm or leg moved half a step behind the right arm or leg. Each forefoot followed the hindfoot on the same side of the body. Elephants and rhinos walk like this today for stability.

228	225	220	215	210	205	200	195	190	185	180	175	170	165	160	155	150

MIDDLE JURASSIC

● The hindfeet of sauropods left large, circular footprints, which shows that a pad of fibrous tissue supported the raised ankle. This tissue provided a broad support for the foot and helped "spring" the foot into the air, thus saving energy.

● Despite their huge size, all sauropods were digitigrade and walked on their fingers and toes. Like later sauropods, Shunosaurus's five fingers pointed out to the side during locomotion, rather than straight ahead.

● A large claw on the thumb may have been used as a weapon, but the other fingers ended in blunt hooves instead of sharp talons.

● All five toes were weight-bearing, with large claws on the first and second toes, and small or absent claws on the third, fourth, and fifth toes. The toe claws also pointed outward, rather than straight ahead.

| 140 | 135 | 130 | 125 | 120 | 115 | 110 | 105 | 100 | 95 | 90 | 85 | 80 | 75 | 70 | 65 MILLION YEARS AGO |

diplodocus *legged dinosaurs*

Diplodocus (double beam) was a famous Late Jurassic sauropod. It moved its 15-ton body around the western areas of North America around 150 million years ago. With an extended neck and tail, it reached 89ft (27m) in length—longer than a tennis court!

● *Diplodocus* had a very long tail and a long neck with a tiny skull. The body was short and compact, and the tail and neck drooped downward.

● V-shaped spines ran down its back. Scientists have calculated that muscles packed between the spines would have only just been strong enough to hold the head up. As the hindlimbs were longer than the forelimbs, the head was held quite close to the ground.

● *Diplodocus* held its limbs directly beneath its body and walked on its fingers and toes. It also held the long bones of the hands and feet in a more vertical position than *Shunosaurus*, meaning that the wrists and ankles were held far from the ground.

● The upper hand bones were arranged in a semicircular arc, and this produced an easily recognizable upside-down U-shaped handprint. The finger and toe bones were reduced to short stumps, tipped with claws or blunt hooves.

228	225	220	215	210	205	200	195	190	185	180	175	170	165	160	155	150

LATE JURASSIC

● The shape of the pencil-like teeth sticking out from the front of the jaws suggests that *Diplodocus* ate leaves, fruits, and seeds from shrubs, ferns, and trees. Since its teeth could not grind its food, it used stones stored in the stomach to grind up what it ate.

● Because *Diplodocus* supported 75 percent of its total bodyweight on its hindlimbs, it may have been able to rear up, balanced by its tail. It is likely that it could raise its head for short periods of time to reach leaves in overhead branches.

● *Diplodocus* could not run, and may not have even been able to manage a fast walk. Its walking speed has been estimated at 7mph (11.5km/h).

● Despite its slow nature, *Diplodocus* used an unusual weapon against predators. Strong muscles at the base of the tail flicked the tiny end tail bones through the air so fast that they sounded like a cracking whip!

| 140 | 135 | 130 | 125 | 120 | 115 | 110 | 105 | 100 | 95 | 90 | 85 | 80 | 75 | 70 | 65 MILLION YEARS AGO |

camarasaurus

Camarasaurus (chambered lizard) was one of the most abundant dinosaurs inhabiting the western North American floodplains in the Late Jurassic period (159–144 million years ago). It lived alongside *Diplodocus*, and, although both animals were herbivorous four-legged sauropods, differences in skull and tooth shape meant that these two dinosaurs fed on different types of plants.

● *Camarasaurus* measured up to 66ft (20m) in length. It was a relatively small sauropod dinosaur, and would have fallen prey to large carnivorous theropods such as *Allosaurus*.

● The column-like arms and legs moved half a step out of phase so that as the back leg was lifted up at the end of a stride, the front leg was being placed on the ground to begin the next step.

● The back was almost horizontal, as the upper arm bones were nearly as long as the thigh bones. In sauropods such as *Diplodocus*, the arm bones were much shorter than the leg bones, and the back sloped downward toward the shoulders.

● *Camarasaurus* bones were much thicker than the ones found on *Diplodocus*, so it probably weighed more (up to 20 ton), despite having weight-reducing "chambers" in its backbone.

228	225	220	215	210	205	200	195	190	185	180	175	170	165	160	155	150

LATE JURASSI

● *Camarasaurus* probably could not rear onto its hindlimbs, as thicker bones and larger forelimbs meant that the front of the body was too heavy to lift off the ground.

● The feet were very solid and had claws on the first three toes. There was only one claw on the hands, placed on the thumbs. The neck and tail were quite short by sauropod standards, although they were very thick.

● Ball-and-socket joints at the base of the neck helped *Camarasaurus* raise its head up to 26ft (8m) off the ground. Long overlapping ribs in the neck restricted side-to-side neck movements.

● *Camarasaurus* had a short but tall skull filled with strong interlocking teeth which could cut against each other to slice through thick twigs and branches. It lived in open conifer forests, where tougher plant food was in plentiful supply.

| 140 | 135 | 130 | 125 | 120 | 115 | 110 | 105 | 100 | 95 | 90 | 85 | 80 | 75 | 70 | 65 MILLION YEARS AGO |

brachiosaurus
four legged dinosaurs

Brachiosaurus was another Late Jurassic giant, taller than a four-story building, and weighed between 35 and 50 tons. It was the only sauropod with arms longer than its legs, hence its name, which means "arm lizard."

● With its long front legs and upright neck, *Brachiosaurus* has been likened to an oversize giraffe. Its neck alone was 30ft (9m) long! Altogether, Brachiosaurus could raise its head at least 38ft (11.5m) into the trees.

● *Brachiosaurus*'s heart needed to be very powerful to pump blood to such a height, and muscular blood vessels and special one-way valves probably helped blood reach the brain.

● *Brachiosaurus* modified its skeleton to help reduce its weight. The neck bones and the ribs were filled with pockets of air to lighten the load. Also, the body is quite narrow and the tail is short.

● Unusually for a sauropod, *Brachiosaurus* supported nearly half its bodyweight on its forelegs (arms) and probably could not rear up on its hindlimbs. Each thumb alone bore a small claw.

228	225	220	215	210	205	200	195	190	185	180	175	170	165	160	155	150

LATE JURASS

● When the arms were brought forward at the beginning of a stride, the elbow bent out to the side slightly, before locking beneath the body at the end of each step. Usually, large animals have their legs directly beneath their bodies to support their weight.

● The hindlimbs were column-like weight-bearing bones that only bent backward and forward like a hinge. The long bones of the foot were held close to the ground, supported by a large, fleshy heel-pad.

● *Brachiosaurus*'s size and weight meant it could not run, and struggled to maintain a fast walk. Its top speed has been estimated at 11mph (18km/h). Fully-grown brachiosaurs evaded attack not by running but by simply being too big to kill.

● It ate by probing its long snout into bristly conifer trees and cropped leaves and branches using its thick, chisel-tipped teeth. Strong neck muscles were responsible for keeping the head up in the trees.

| 140 | 135 | 130 | 125 | 120 | 115 | 110 | 105 | 100 | 95 | 90 | 85 | 80 | 75 | 70 | 65 MILLION YEARS AGO |

saltasaurus
four legged dinosaurs

Saltasaurus (lizard from Salta province) belonged to a group of sauropod dinosaurs known as "titanosaurs" (gigantic lizards). Titanosaurs lived all over the world, especially during the Cretaceous period, but *Saltasaurus* itself is only known from the Late Cretaceous of Argentina in South America.

● Measuring 39ft (12m) in length, *Saltasaurus* was a relatively small sauropod dinosaur. It lived among lowland trees and ferns around 73–65 million years ago. It probably weighed around 25 tons.

● Like *Diplodocus*, it possessed a long, whiplash tail. To provide further defense, its back and sides had plate-sized shields of bone and interlocking pea-sized bony nodules. Bony spines protruded from the top of each neck vertebra.

● *Saltasaurus*, like many titanosaurs, held its legs slightly out to the side of its body. The hip socket pointed sideway and downward, and this angled the whole thigh bone (femur) sideway from the hip.

● The knee joint was shaped so that the tibia and fibula (shinbones) and the long bones of the foot were held vertical to the ground. It had five toes, but only the inner three toes bore claws.

| 228 | 225 | 220 | 215 | 210 | 205 | 200 | 195 | 190 | 185 | 180 | 175 | 170 | 165 | 160 | 155 | 150 |

● The rib cage was very broad, and *Saltasaurus* had a large, barrel-shaped belly. Bony spurs stuck out sideway from the hips onto which the muscles that supported its large stomach were attached. Muscles to pull the hindlimbs forward were attached here too.

● The shoulders were also broad and the arms were normally bent slightly at the elbows. Titanosaur footprints show that the hands were not placed as far apart as the feet. The elbows and knees were very flexible.

● Unusually, *Saltasaurus* had a flexible body. The base of its tail was also flexible and built to support the body if *Saltasaurus* reared onto its hindlimbs. It may have done this to protect its young from attack, or to reach leaves on high branches.

● Footprint evidence shows a titanosaur like *Saltasaurus* either walking carefully over a slippery surface, or walking bipedally at 1mph (1.8km/h). Walking on normal surface on four legs, it could reach speeds of 11mph (18km/h).

| 140 | 135 | 130 | 125 | 120 | 115 | 110 | 105 | 100 | 95 | 90 | 85 | 80 | 75 | 70 | 65 | MILLION YEARS AGO |

LATE CRETACEOUS

euoplocephalus

four legged dinosaurs

Euoplocephalus (well-armored head) was a quadrupedal ornithischian dinosaur. Its body was covered in protective plates of bone and a bony club tipped the end of the tail. It lived in North American woodland during the last few million years of the dinosaurs.

● *Euoplocephalus* was up to 23ft (7m) long. The upper surface of its body, including neck and head, was covered in large, hinged, knobbly plates of bone and bony conical horns. This protective covering made it very heavy, weighing up to 2.5 tons.

● *Euoplocephalus* used its beak and simple teeth to crop and slice low-lying plants. Food was then passed to the barrel-shaped gut for digestion. The stomach could hold lots of sloshy fermenting plant matter, which also added to the weight of the animal.

● *Euoplocephalus* walked on arms and legs that were stocky and short, to resist bending under the weight of its wide, heavy body. Footprint and anatomical evidence has shown that the legs were tucked well underneath the body.

● The hindlimbs were held straight beneath the body and moved in a parasagittal way. Four hooved toes faced slightly outward as the animal walked. The arms were usually held straight, but seemed to bend outward slightly at the elbow as it moved.

228	225	220	215	210	205	200	195	190	185	180	175	170	165	160	155	150

● The arm and leg muscles were powerful, although not designed to move the arms and legs quickly. However, for such a bulky animal, *Euoplocephalus* was actually quite agile and moved more like a rhino than the slow-moving tortoise it resembles.

● *Euoplocephalus* could move at around 4¹/₂mph (7km/h) and might only have managed a slow trot for short periods of time. It was therefore slower than some sauropods and other quadrupedal ornithischians such as *Triceratops*.

● *Euoplocephalus* had developed the end of its tail into a bony club. In most dinosaurs, the caudofemoralis muscle was used to pull the thigh bone (femur) backward during walking, but it was also used by *Euoplocephalus* to swing the tail club from side to side.

● A sharp swipe of the strengthened tail could have seriously damaged the lower legs of a hungry predator such as *Tyrannosaurus rex*. *Euoplocephalus*'s body armor was also a useful protection against attack.

stegosaurus

Stegosaurus (roofed lizard) is famous for the huge bony plates that lined its back and tail. It lived in the Late Jurassic period in North America about 146 million years ago and reached up to 30ft (9m) long, weighing in at up to two tons.

● The largest plates were 3ft (1m) tall but were too thin and soft to act as useful armor. It is possible that the plates were used in a male ranking system. The Stegosaurus with the best plates took the lead over the rest of the group.

● The plates could also have been used to control body temperature, since they contained a network of blood vessels. When passed close to the surface, blood could be heated up by the sun, or alternatively, cooled by a breeze.

● Stegosaurus's limbs were held pillar-like beneath the body. The hindlimbs were much longer than the powerful forelimbs, and the thigh bone (femur) was especially long. It could only move at 3¹/₂–4¹/₂mph (6–7km/h), equivalent to human walking speed.

● The bones of its hindlimbs were more slender than those of the forelimbs, even though Stegosaurus rested 80 percent of its bulk on its hindfeet. The small head was held close to the ground.

| 228 | 225 | 220 | 215 | 210 | 205 | 200 | 195 | 190 | 185 | 180 | 175 | 170 | 165 | 160 | 155 | 150 |

LATE JURASSIC

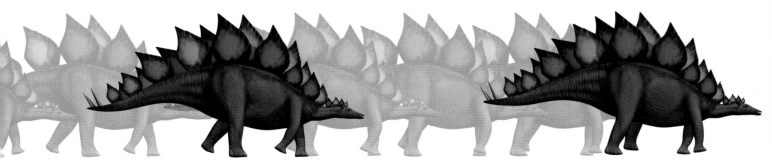

● Because the legs were so long and as the center of mass was balanced around the hips, *Stegosaurus* was probably able to rear up onto its hind legs from where it could reach plants and trees 20ft (6m) above the ground.

● However, *Stegosaurus* lived in the time of the giant sauropods *Camarasaurus* and *Brachiosaurus*. These tall animals probably fed from higher branches leaving low-lying plants and ferns for *Stegosaurus* to munch on.

● *Stegosaurus* had a muscular tail that was flexible along its length and had four sharp spikes at its tip. It could swing its tail from side to side using modified leg muscles.

● When under attack, *Stegosaurus* may have used its long hindlimbs and short forelimbs to quickly spin its body around so that the spiny tail could be better positioned to attack to the spindly legs of enemies such as the meat-eating theropod, *Allosaurus*.

| 140 | 135 | 130 | 125 | 120 | 115 | 110 | 105 | 100 | 95 | 90 | 85 | 80 | 75 | 70 | 65 | MILLION YEARS AGO |

triceratops

four legged dinosaurs

Triceratops (three-horned face) lived among the last of the dinosaurs in the late Cretaceous period about 68–65 million years ago. Its remains are found in western North America and Canada, where it lived on coastal plains along the shores of an ancient inland sea.

● *Triceratops* is one of the most popular and familiar dinosaurs. 30ft (9m) long, its tail was quite short as it was not needed to counter-balance the weight of the body. It was still a large, barrel-shaped animal that weighed up to six tons.

● The skull was very heavy: it was 6½ft (2m) long and had three bony horns and a solid bony frill that extended over the neck. As well as for defense, male *Triceratops* may have used their horns to fight each other for females or territory, like modern-day deer.

● The huge skull meant that the forelimbs carried over 50 percent of the animal's weight; normally the hindlimbs take most of the strain. The hindlimbs were held directly beneath the body and were stout, pillar-like, and much longer than the forelimbs.

● Scientists are still unsure about how *Triceratops* moved its forelimbs. Some think that the upper arm bone (humerus) was held out to the side of the body and the elbows were bent. There is evidence that huge chest muscles aided this "press-up" posture.

228 225 220 215 210 205 200 195 190 185 180 175 170 165 160 155 150

● Sprawling the limbs out to the sides kept the body stable when fighting with the horns. In this position, *Triceratops* could manage a slow run, but could not gallop, with a top speed of 16mph (26km/h).

● Other researchers argue that the rib cage was narrower than usually reconstructed. This brings the legs underneath the body while keeping the elbows and shoulder joints locked together. The elbow is now only slightly bent.

● Researchers in favor of this more upright posture also argue that sprawling lizards move their backbone from side to side with each step, but *Triceratops* could not move like this because its rib cage and backbone were tightly fused together.

● *Triceratops* ate tough vegetation such as palms and ferns. It used its pointed beak to pluck stems and branches, which were then shredded by rows of sharp teeth.

140	135	130	125	120	115	110	105	100	95	90	85	80	75	70	65 MILLION YEARS AGO

LATE CRETACEOUS

two- & four-legged dinosaurs

plateosaurus two & four-legged dinosaurs

Plateosaurus (flat lizard) was an early saurischian dinosaur. It belongs to a group of dinosaurs known as prosauropods, which were closely related to the sauropods. *Plateosaurus* lived 220 million years ago, not long after the dawn of the dinosaurs. It was one of the first really large dinosaurs and reached up to 26ft (8m) in length.

● *Plateosaurus* was one of the first plant-eating dinosaurs and lived on the lush floodplains of Europe and Greenland, where vegetation was plentiful. On all fours, it fed on plants growing close to the ground.

● *Plateosaurus* had a small head lined with plant-shredding saw-edged teeth. Some scientists thought that these teeth were used to cut up meat, but *Plateosaurus*'s long, barrel-shaped belly shows that a large plant-fermenting gut was present.

● The tail was long and heavy at its base, and both the fore and hindlimbs were powerful. Since its hindlimbs were longer than the forelimbs and it had a tail for balancing, *Plateosaurus* could have reared onto its back legs to feed from the treetops.

● Smaller prosauropods could run smoothly on just their hind legs. Larger prosauropods such as *Plateosaurus* may have been able to run bipedally for short periods of time only. On two legs, its head could reach 10–13ft (3–4m) off the ground.

228	225	220	215	210	205	200	195	190	185	180	175	170	165	160	155	150

LATE TRIASSIC

● *Plateosaurus* moved its limbs in a parasagittal plane, and its thighs slanted away from its body slightly. As well as having a short ilium (hip bone), the muscles that moved the legs were still being developed. The hands and feet were long, broad, and supportive.

● *Plateosaurus* had four clawed toes and five fingers. The outer two fingers were reduced in size, and the first three fingers all bore long, narrow claws. The thumb claw was particularly large and probably needed to be held off the ground during locomotion.

● *Plateosaurus* may have used its finger claws to tear up roots, shrubs, and insect molds, and also to hook branches while rearing up on its hind legs. The thumb claw may have been used as a weapon against predators such as the crocodile-like *Saurosuchus*.

● *Plateosaurus* was capable of trotting at around 11mph (18km/h). Because it had a long back, it may have bounded along on all fours, moving its front and hindlimbs together, as cheetahs and some dogs do today.

| 140 | 135 | 130 | 125 | 120 | 115 | 110 | 105 | 100 | 95 | 90 | 85 | 80 | 75 | 70 | 65 | MILLION YEARS AGO |

iguanodon *four-legged dinosaurs*

Iguanodon was a large Early Cretaceous herbivorous dinosaur which lived in Europe, Asia, and North America. It appears that *Iguanodon* preferred to live on fertile low-lying plains, criss-crossed by rivers and streams. Here it could find giant tree ferns, conifers, horsetails, and cycads to eat.

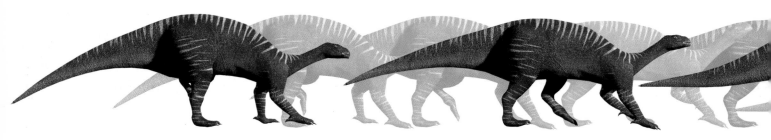

● *Iguanodon* belonged to a group of dinosaurs known as "ornithopods." All ornithopods were ornithischian dinosaurs with a backward-facing pubis bone in the hip.

● Trackways show that *Iguanodon* walked on all fours at least some of the time. The trackways show that either its arms bent out slightly at the elbow compared to its hind legs, or that the body was slightly wider at the chest than the hips.

● The spine was held horizontally, bringing the arms closer to the ground, so Iguanodon could walk on either two or four legs. The tail was also held horizontally away from the body, above the ground.

● With a large, horse-like head and heavy tail, the body was likely to sag over the hips, but bony rods strengthened the spine. The hind legs were longer than the arms and three-toed feet supported the body. Each toe ended in a long bony hoof.

228	225	220	215	210	205	200	195	190	185	180	175	170	165	160	155	150

● The arms were roughly three-quarters the length of the legs. The middle three fingers of the hand were tipped with blunt hooves and could bend backward to support the body while walking on all fours. The fifth finger was thin and flexible.

● The thumb could not touch the other fingers of the hand and was held out sideway. The end of the thumb was modified into a large conical spike that was used as a weapon. Predators such as *Neovenator* needed to be careful when launching an attack.

● *Iguanodon* reached 30–33ft (9–10m) long and weighed up to two tons. Researchers have estimated *Iguanodon* could move at around 7–10mph (11–16km/h), possibly roaming the countryside in large herds.

● At first, scientists thought *Iguanodon* looked like a heavy rhino, lumbering along on all fours. When hundreds of skeletons were later found in Belgium, scientists incorrectly thought it walked upright on two legs, propped up by a heavy tail that rested on the ground.

| 140 | 135 | 130 | 125 | 120 | 115 | 110 | 105 | 100 | 95 | 90 | 85 | 80 | 75 | 70 | 65 MILLION YEARS AGO |

EARLY CRETACEOUS

maiasaura

Maiasaura (good mother lizard) was a "duck-billed" ornithopod dinosaur. It was a gentle herbivore that cared for its young in densely packed nesting grounds. These nesting areas could be found 80 to 73 million years ago in western parts of North America.

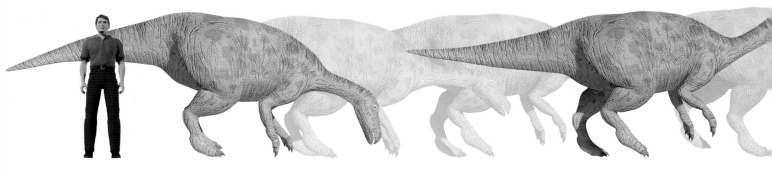

● *Maiasaura* fossils of all ages have been discovered, from newborn babies to fully-grown adults. Using these fossils, scientists have been able to investigate how long *Maiasaura* babies spent in the nest and how fast these dinosaurs grew.

● At hatching, *Maiasaura* babies were 19½in (50cm) long. Their bones were slim and their limbs were long and spindly. They had arched backbones and U-shaped necks similar to the adults. *Maiasaura* babies had weak legs and could not walk or run properly.

● *Maiasaura* babies could not gather food themselves, yet their teeth were worn down, showing that they had begun to eat tough plant matter, brought to the nest by an attentive parent. Fossilized leaves, seeds, and fruits have been found in nests.

● *Maiasaura* hatchlings remained in the nest for up to two months. During this time, the babies grew very fast, doubling in length in just four weeks. Their legs became stronger and the hips formed a solid connection to the backbone.

| 228 | 225 | 220 | 215 | 210 | 205 | 200 | 195 | 190 | 185 | 180 | 175 | 170 | 165 | 160 | 155 | 150 |

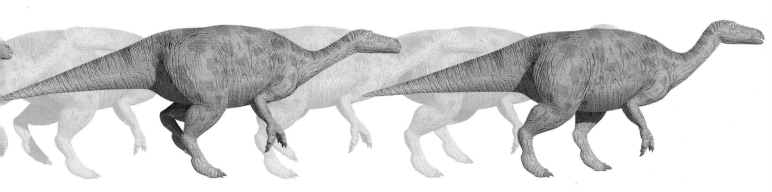

● Young *Maiasaura* probably ventured further from the nest, foraging for food under the watchful eye of a parent. When *Maiasaura* reached about 5ft (1.5m) in length, the size of a large dog, it was ready to leave the nest and join the rest of the herd.

● *Maiasaura* continued to grow very fast until two years of age, when they were around 10ft (3m) long. *Maiasaura* reached adulthood at around four to six years old. Their limbs were short and robust and their legs were longer than their arms.

● *Maiasaura* stood and walked on all fours, reaching 19¹/₂–26ft (6–8m) long, yet probably used only two legs to move quickly, at around 9–12mph (14–20km/h).

● *Maiasaura* appear to have returned to nest in the same place every year, with up to 10,000 animals nesting together. To provide food for the whole herd, they would leave the nesting site when the young were strong enough and migrate to find untouched forest.

| 140 | 135 | 130 | 125 | 120 | 115 | 110 | 105 | 100 | 95 | 90 | 85 | 80 | 75 | 70 | 65 MILLION YEARS AGO |

LATE CRETACEOUS

two-legged dinosaurs

hypsilophodon

Hypsilophodon (high ridge tooth) was a small Early Cretaceous dinosaur. A speedy bipedal herbivore, it lived in England, Spain, and possibly North America around 125 to 119 million years ago.

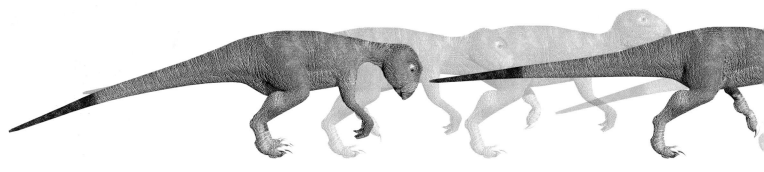

- *Hypsilophodon* is named after its ridged, leaf-shaped teeth. Cheek pouches prevented food falling from the mouth while the sharp, interlocking teeth sliced through tough plant matter. It also had a nipping beak, useful for roots and shoots.

- *Hypsilophodon* reached a maximum of 6½ft (2m) long and probably weighed only 55lb (25kg), about as same as a medium-sized dog. The shape of its skeleton tells us that *Hypsilophodon* was a lightly built dinosaur, designed for speed.

- Its arms were quite short and the five fingers were adapted for grasping shoots and stems rather than running. *Hypsilophodon* ran only on its back legs, which were long, slender, and lightweight.

- The relative lengths of the thigh, shin, and toe bones show that it was a very cursorial dinosaur. The long bones of the feet were especially elongated. Large, powerful thigh muscles ensured that the legs could move backward and forward quickly and powerfully.

| 228 | 225 | 220 | 215 | 210 | 205 | 200 | 195 | 190 | 185 | 180 | 175 | 170 | 165 | 160 | 155 | 150 |

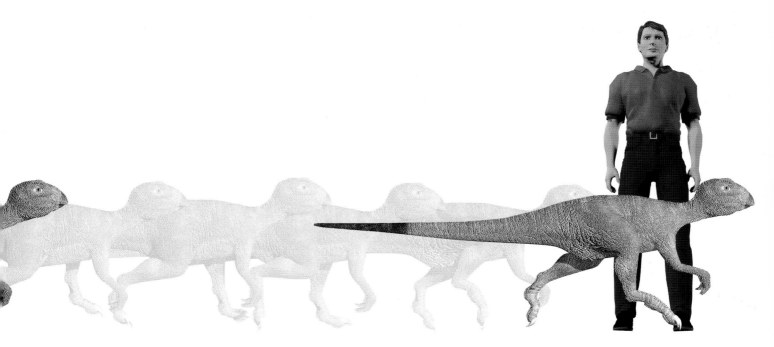

● *Hypsilophodon* may have reached speeds of 20mph (32km/h). This would make it a very fast runner, albeit only for short periods of time—though long enough to escape from predators such as the meat-eater, *Altispinax*.

● *Hypsilophodon*'s body was held close to the ground and was carefully balanced at the hips by the long tail.

● The tail was held as a rigid rod that worked as a rudder, helping *Hypsilophodon* change direction quickly. It also acted as a stabilizer, keeping the animal balanced while running fast or covering uneven ground.

● Scientists have compared *Hypsilophodon* to small antelope, such as the gazelle, found in Africa today. Like antelope, it fed on shoots and leaves, and used speed rather than large size or armor to escape predators.

| 140 | 135 | 130 | 125 | 120 | 115 | 110 | 105 | 100 | 95 | 90 | 85 | 80 | 75 | 70 | 65 MILLION YEARS AGO |

EARLY CRETACEOUS

pachycephalosaurus

Pachycephalosaurus (thick-headed reptile) was an herbivorous dinosaur that lived in North American forests at the end of the Cretaceous period, 68 to 65 million years ago. Its most distinctive feature was a huge dome on top of its head.

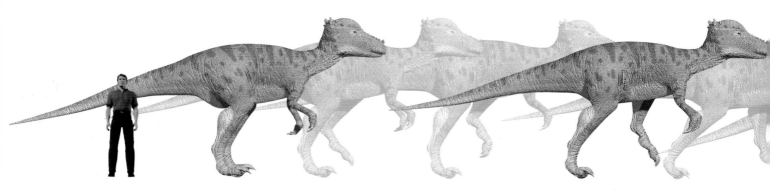

● The dome was made from 10in- (25cm) thick, solid bone. Scientists have long speculated about the function of the huge dome, which was probably not used for protection from predators, as the rest of the body was free from bony armor and open to attack.

● Different shaped domes may have enabled different bone-headed dinosaurs to recognize members of their own species, but this is only a theory.

● Most researchers agree than the dome was used in fights between members of the same species. Like modern day mountain sheep and goats, males used the dome in contests over their rank, and for access to females for mating.

● During fights, *Pachycephalosaurus* probably held its backbone horizontally. The head was fixed to the neck in such as way that the dome faced directly forward like a battering ram when the backbone was straight.

| 228 | 225 | 220 | 215 | 210 | 205 | 200 | 195 | 190 | 185 | 180 | 175 | 170 | 165 | 160 | 155 | 150 |

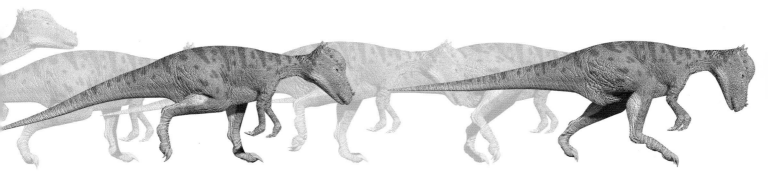

● Once the target was pinpointed using its forward-facing eyes, *Pachycephalosaurus* ran toward its rival, possibly reaching speeds of up to 9mph (14.5km/h).

● The rest of the body was designed so that it didn't hurt itself while head-butting a rival. The neck was short, strong, and wide, and stiffened bony rods ran along the backbone and tail. Specially constructed vertebrae also prevented the backbone from twisting.

● *Pachycephalosaurus* was fully bipedal: the legs were much longer than the arms. During normal walking, the neck was bent upward and the head faced forward.

● The tail was large and rigid and acted as a counter-balance to the heavy head. The hips were broad so the feet were placed far apart on the ground, keeping the animal stable, useful during fights.

| 140 | 135 | 130 | 125 | 120 | 115 | 110 | 105 | 100 | 95 | 90 | 85 | 80 | 75 | 70 | 65 MILLION YEARS AGO |

LATE CRETACEOUS

herrerasaurus

two legged dinosaurs

Herrerasaurus (Herrera's lizard) was a meat-eating dinosaur from what is now north-western Argentina, South America. *Herrerasaurus* comes from the Late Triassic period 228 million years ago, making it one of the earliest known dinosaurs.

● *Herrerasaurus* is one of a small group of very primitive dinosaurs, so primitive that some scientists think that it is not a dinosaur at all! Either way, it gives us a very good idea of what the earliest dinosaurs and their direct ancestors looked like.

● *Herrerasaurus* was bipedal. In fact, the ancestor of all dinosaurs (saurischians and ornithischians) was a bipedal creature. *Herrerasaurus* had quite short arms of which the hands formed a large part.

● There were five fingers on each hand, the first three fingers with claws, the other fingers very small. Saurischian dinosaurs have this feature which may link *Herrerasaurus* with this group. As *Herrerasaurus* had hollow limb bones, it may actually be a very early theropod.

● A characteristic of all dinosaurs is that the three hip bones, the ilium, ischium and pubis, do not fully meet in the center of the hip, leaving an opening into which the head of the thigh bone (femur) slots.

228	225	220	215	210	205	200	195	190	185	180	175	170	165	160	155	150

LATE TRIASSIC

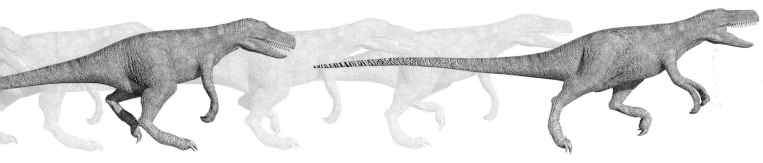

● *Herrerasaurus* hips have this characteristic opening, although there is some debate whether the opening was fully formed or not. Its legs were not pillar-like beneath the body, but slanted slightly outward.

● The feet had five long toes. The first and last toes were reduced to the extent that the first toe barely touched the ground, and the fifth toe didn't reach at all.

● *Herrerasaurus* lived in a humid woodland environment, surrounded by rivers, lakes, and bogs. It used grasping hands; sharp, curved, serrated teeth; and a flexible lower jaw to catch and eat prey such as the common pig-like rhynchosaurs.

● *Herrerasaurus* was probably not a fast runner, although being two-legged, it could be quite agile. It grew 10–16ft (3–5m) long, weighed 550–660lb (250–300kg), and its legs were about 3ft (1m) long.

| 140 | 135 | 130 | 125 | 120 | 115 | 110 | 105 | 100 | 95 | 90 | 85 | 80 | 75 | 70 | 65 MILLION YEARS AGO |

coelophysis *two-legged dinosaurs*

Coelophysis (hollow form) lived in the Late Triassic about 227 to 223 million years ago. Its bones have been found in western North America, and what may be *Coelophysis* footprints have been found in rocks as far away as East Greenland.

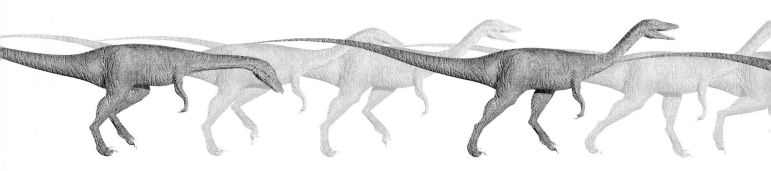

● *Coelophysis* was a bipedal, carnivorous animal, living on lizards, insects, and fish. It measured up to 10ft (3m) long, but because its bones were hollow and thin-walled, it may have weighed only 33–66lb (15–30kg).

● By studying footprints preserved in mud, scientists can tell that *Coelophysis* had five toes, but only three were used during everyday walking. The first toe was held off the ground, while the fifth toe was reduced to a tiny splint of bone.

● At the beginning of a stride, the three toes were splayed outward. Toward the end of the stride, the three toes were brought together and lifted upward with the long bones of the foot (the metatarsals) held vertically.

● The metatarsals were fused to each other and to small ankle bones. Other large ankle bones called the "astragalus" and "calcaneum" were fused to the shinbones to create a stable, hinge-like ankle joint.

| 228 | 225 | 220 | 215 | 210 | 205 | 200 | 195 | 190 | 185 | 180 | 175 | 170 | 165 | 160 | 155 | 150 |

LATE TRIASSIC

● The hip bones were fused tightly together, and one of the muscles responsible for pulling the legs forward during locomotion was large and powerful.

● The shin and thigh bones are long, meaning *Coelophysis* was definitely cursorial and may have reached a top speed of 22½mph (36km/h). Everyday speed was probably much slower.

● *Coelophysis* used speed and agility to catch prey, aided by a long, curved neck, a sharp-toothed skull, and grasping hands. *Coelophysis* had a strong, thumb-like first digit, two long clawed fingers, and two further fingers, which were just stumps of bone.

● Unfortunately, *Coelophysis* put these useful tools to terrible use: some adult fossils have the remains of young *Coelophysis* preserved in their guts, meaning these dinosaurs were cannibals!

| 140 | 135 | 130 | 125 | 120 | 115 | 110 | 105 | 100 | 95 | 90 | 85 | 80 | 75 | 70 | 65 MILLION YEARS AGO |

carnotaurus

Carnotaurus (meat-eating bull) was a 7.5m (24½ft) bipedal carnivorous dinosaur. It lived in the mid-Cretaceous period in Argentina about 113 to 91 million years ago. It is named after an unusual pair of bony bull-like horns extending from its skull.

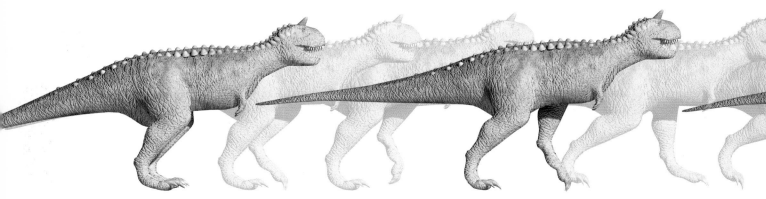

● In the Jurassic period, South America became separated from the other southern continents of Australia, Africa, and Antarctica. *Carnotaurus* existed in South America, while its relatives have been found as far apart as India and Madagascar.

● *Carnotaurus* weighed up to one ton and measured 7ft (2.2m) at hip height. It had a short but high skull, capped by two stout, blunt horns that may have been used in fights with other male carnotaurs or used to signal to females.

● *Carnotaurus* lived on dry plains. Long, slim legs suggest it was quite cursorial. Three strong toes touched the ground, while the first toe was elevated to the side. The ankle was held off the ground and the thigh bone (femur) was short and stocky.

● The tail was long and thin. The ilium bone was not stretched as far forward and backward along the backbone as in some later theropods. This meant that muscles extending the knees and pulling the thigh bone (femur) forward were not as well developed.

| 228 | 225 | 220 | 215 | 210 | 205 | 200 | 195 | 190 | 185 | 180 | 175 | 170 | 165 | 160 | 155 | 150 |

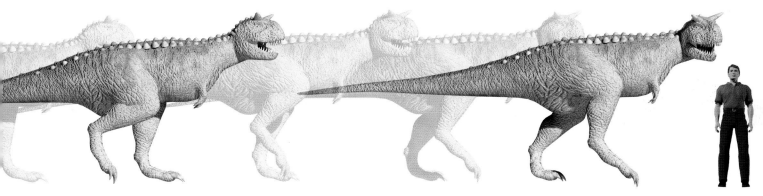

● *Carnotaurus* was still probably a competent runner, possibly reaching speeds of 19mph (30km/h).

● *Carnotaurus* had a narrow snout, but its eyes faced forward slightly, giving it the benefit of forward—rather than side—vision, allowing it to pinpoint prey with some accuracy. Ambush tactics and bursts of high speed may have also helped it catch its prey.

● *Carnotaurus* had four fingers, but the arms were so small that they were useless for catching prey. Instead, the skull may have been flexible, enabling *Carnotaurus* to wrap its jaws around its prey.

● Long, delicate teeth and a fast jaw action suggest that *Carnotaurus* may have preyed on smaller animals and scavenged carcasses.

| 140 | 135 | 130 | 125 | 120 | 115 | 110 | 105 | 100 | 95 | 90 | 85 | 80 | 75 | 70 | 65 MILLION YEARS AGO |

MID-CRETACEOUS

megalosaurus

two-legged dinosaurs

Megalosaurus (big lizard) was a meat-eating theropod dinosaur. Its remains have been found in England and France in rocks from the Middle Jurassic around 163 million years ago. It was about 23–29½ft (7–9m) long, walked on two legs and may have weighed over 1.5 tons.

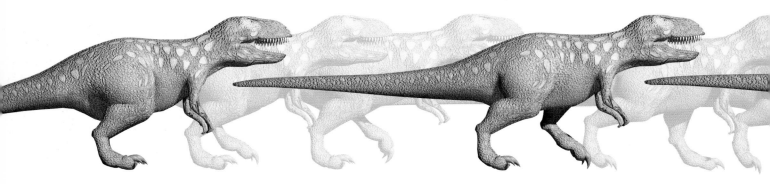

● *Megalosaurus* was the first dinosaur to be scientifically named and described, in 1824. Fossilized bones, including a portion of the lower jaw, with teeth, and parts of the backbone, hips, and legs were discovered near Oxford, England.

● These early remains were named *Megalosaurus* by William Buckland, a church minister and scientist at Oxford University. Dinosaurs were not known to exist at this time, and scientists thought *Megalosaurus* was a giant four-legged land-dwelling lizard.

● *Megalosaurus* had a large head with jaws lined with quite stout but sharp teeth. It had short, strong arms ending in a three-fingered hand and long, muscular legs. Each foot ended in three toes tipped with a sharp claw, as well as a smaller extra toe.

● *Megalosaurus* lived around woodland along the coast of a sea that covered parts of England and France at that time. It walked at about 4mph (6.8km/h), about the same speed as a human jogging slowly.

228	225	220	215	210	205	200	195	190	185	180	175	170	165	160	155	150

MIDDLE JURASSIC

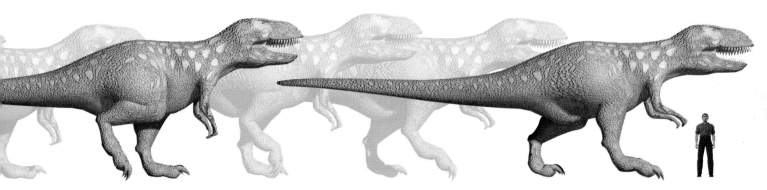

● *Megalosaurus* 's feet were placed quite widely apart, meaning the legs were sprawled outward slightly to the side, unusual for dinosaurs. This would place large bending stresses on the leg bones, but would make *Megalosaurus* more stable on two legs.

● Amazingly, one trackway shows *Megalosaurus* breaking into a run, with its stride length increasing from 9ft (2.7m) to 18½ft (5.65m) and speed increasing to 18mph (29km/h)— only slightly slower than the fastest human sprinters!

● When running, it brought its legs underneath its body and its feet pointed forward, rather than the inward-pointing position it used when walking. This is the only known example of a large bipedal dinosaur using different leg positions to walk and run.

● It is not known how long *Megalosaurus* could keep running, as the trackway is only 115ft (35m) long. However, it is by far the fastest large theropod dinosaur, beating *T.rex* and *Allosaurus*.

140   135   130   125   120   115   110   105   100   95   90   85   80   75   70   65   MILLION YEARS AGO

giganotosaurus

Measuring up to 47½ft (14.5m) long, and weighing around eight tons, *Giganotosaurus* (giant southern lizard) terrorized most of the animals trying to live and survive on the mid-Cretaceous floodplains of southern South America.

● When it was discovered in 1994, the bipedal theropod *Giganotosaurus* succeeded *T.rex* as the largest land-based carnivorous animal.

● *Giganotosaurus* bones were actually more lightly built than *T.rex* ones, but even so, each three-toed foot supported more than four tons of bodyweight with every step.

● The caudofemoralis muscle, the powerhouse of locomotion, ran from the thigh bone (femur) to halfway down the tail. When this muscle contracted, the leg shifted backward as the body was pushed forward over the hips.

● There are no recorded trackways for this dinosaur, so theoretical estimates have been made about its speed. Some scientists say that *Giganotosaurus* was about as athletic as an elephant. If this is correct, it could walk fast, but could not run.

| 228 | 225 | 220 | 215 | 210 | 205 | 200 | 195 | 190 | 185 | 180 | 175 | 170 | 165 | 160 | 155 | 150 |

● Other scientists say that *Giganotosaurus* could reach speeds of 31 1/2mph (50km/h). This is very fast for such a large animal and may have meant that falling over could have caused serious injury or death.

● The hip joint is 12ft (3.7m) off the ground, meaning *Giganotosaurus* could take very long strides and reach quite a speed without actually breaking into a run.

● Scientists in Argentina have uncovered the remains of several *Giganotosaurus*-like animals. The group consists of two large individuals and two or three smaller animals that may have been a family, hunting together for food.

● A pack of giganotosaurs would have been able to attack enormous armored sauropods, such as the 100-ton *Argentinosaurus*, using their 6ft (1.8m) long skulls—equipped with 8in (20cm) jagged cutting teeth—to slice into their prey.

| 140 | 135 | 130 | 125 | 120 | 115 | 110 | 105 | 100 | 95 | 90 | 85 | 80 | 75 | 70 | 65 | MILLION YEARS AGO |

MID-CRETACEOUS

baryonyx

Back in the Early Cretaceous, around 125 million years ago, a large system of floodplains
and rivers crossed south-east England. The ground was swampy and the climate was subtropical.
Baryonyx (heavy claw) lived here, a large, bipedal carnivorous dinosaur—with a difference.

● *Baryonyx* was a "tetanuran" theropod dinosaur. It was up to 39ft (12m) long and weighed 1.5–2 tons fully grown. It supported its body on sturdy legs, ending in three-toed digitigrade feet.

● The legs were not built for speed and do not show any special adaptation. Only when the rest of the body is considered, particularly the skull and arms, does it become apparent that *Baryonyx* was a very unusual dinosaur.

● Unlike other tetanuran theropods like *Allosaurus* and *T.rex*, *Baryonyx* wasn't so interested in attacking other dinosaurs for food. Instead, it would rather hook a tasty fish out of a river with its claws or sniff out a fresh carcass to eat.

● The skull of *Baryonyx* was long, low, and narrow, like that of a crocodile. The teeth were peg-like stabbers rather than slicers. *Baryonyx* had twice as many lower jaw teeth than other theropods, and a circle of larger teeth protruded from the tips of its jaws.

| 228 | 225 | 220 | 215 | 210 | 205 | 200 | 195 | 190 | 185 | 180 | 175 | 170 | 165 | 160 | 155 | 150 |

● Fish were scooped up in the long jaws, or grasped using the incredibly strong shoulders and arms. Early Cretaceous fish could reach up to 10ft (3m) long—an excellent food source for a large animal like *Baryonyx*.

● Huge claws up to 12in (30cm) long on the thumb-like first digit helped *Baryonyx* catch fish. Fish scales and teeth were actually found inside the rib cage of *Baryonyx*, proving the point.

● *Iguanodon* bones were also found in the belly, but it may have just been feeding on a carcass. In fact, *Baryonyx*'s nostrils were positioned further back on the snout than usual, enabling it to dine inside a carcass or hold its snout under water, and still breathe.

● Finding a carcass needed stamina, not speed, so it was probably not a fast dinosaur. *Baryonyx* offers a useful reminder that scientists sometimes have to look beyond the shape of the legs and hips to gain an idea of how dinosaurs moved.

| 140 | 135 | 130 | 125 | 120 | 115 | 110 | 105 | 100 | 95 | 90 | 85 | 80 | 75 | 70 | 65 MILLION YEARS AGO |

EARLY CRETACEOUS

compsognathus

two legged dinosaurs

Not all dinosaurs were large. The Late Jurassic bipedal dinosaur *Compsognathus* (elegant jaw) only grew to the size of a turkey. 150 million years ago this small dinosaur could be found scurrying through low-lying vegetation along the shore of an ancient European desert island.

● *Compsognathus* was 4¹/₂ft (1.4m) long, measured only 9in (23cm) at the hip, and may have weighed only 6¹/₂lb (3kg). Despite its small size, it was cursorial. The whole skeleton was small and light, and the limb bones were thin-walled and hollow.

● *Compsognathus* was an early member of a large group of theropod dinosaurs called "coelurosaurs," or hollow-tail lizards.

● Its ankle was held well off the ground, the whole foot was extremely long, and muscles used for locomotion were well-developed. As in most theropods, three toes and a tiny raised first toe were present. A long, slender tail aided balancing.

● *Compsognathus* was a swift runner for its size, capable of reaching speeds of up to 10mph (16km/h). In fact, the most agile of all dinosaurs were probably small bipedal creatures like *Compsognathus*, measuring less than 3ft (1m) tall at the hip.

228	225	220	215	210	205	200	195	190	185	180	175	170	165	160	155	150

LATE JURASSI

● Because it was a small animal, it could change from a walk to a trot or run at a fairly low speed. To keep running, it needed to take about four strides per second. By increasing the number of strides per second, it could run even faster!

● *Compsognathus* had a long, lightly built skull full of small sharp teeth. It relied on a diet of insects, small mammals, and other vertebrates. One *Compsognathus* fossil preserved the remains of its last meal—a tiny lizard called *Bavarisaurus*.

● To be able to catch speedy lizards, *Compsognathus* needed a combination of good acceleration, sharp eyesight, and quick reactions. Its small size, light frame, fast-moving legs, and ability to run at low speed helped to increase its agility.

● *Compsognathus* could probably break into a run from a standing start and quickly reach high speed, while side-stepping obstacles with ease.

| 140 | 135 | 130 | 125 | 120 | 115 | 110 | 105 | 100 | 95 | 90 | 85 | 80 | 75 | 70 | 65 MILLION YEARS AGO |

sinosauropteryx

Sinosauropteryx (Chinese lizard wing) lived in the Early Cretaceous around 125 to 119 million years ago in north-eastern China. It is the earliest known theropod dinosaur to have feather-like structures on its body. Only a few fossils are known, all found in what was a lake—where gentle currents and the slow build-up of sand and mud helped preserve the feathery filaments in some detail.

● *Sinosauropteryx* was a small bipedal theropod about 3ft (1m) long, weighing only 6½–11lb (3–5kg). A narrow snout lined with tiny, sharp teeth tells us that *Sinosauropteryx* lived on a diet of insects and small lizards and mammals.

● *Sinosauropteryx* lived in the Early Cretaceous in Asia, yet was very similar in size and shape to the Late Jurassic European theropod *Compsognathus*. Both dinosaurs have short arms, long tails, and thinly constructed skulls.

● *Sinosauropteryx* was probably an agile, fast-moving animal, darting along lakeshores in search of prey. Preserved inside the belly of one *Sinosauropteryx* specimen were the jawbones of a primitive mammal— its last meal before death.

● *Sinosauropteryx* feathers were not used for flying. In fact, they were useless at achieving any kind of lift. Modern bird feathers are formed from strong, branching filaments, tightly locked together.

| 228 | 225 | 220 | 215 | 210 | 205 | 200 | 195 | 190 | 185 | 180 | 175 | 170 | 165 | 160 | 155 | 150 |

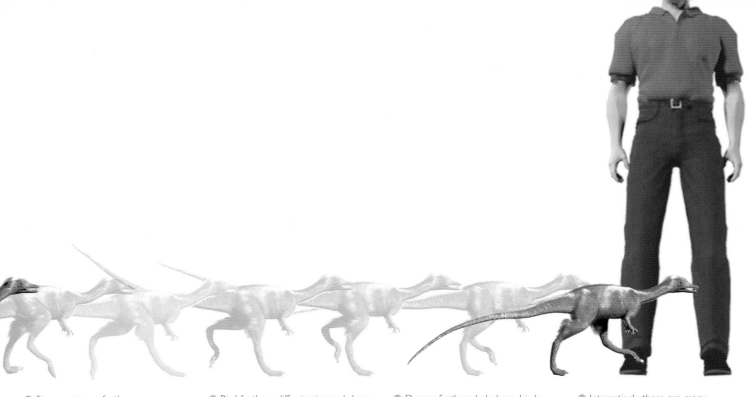

● *Sinosauropteryx* feathers were composed mainly from a hollow central quill with a few, noninterlocking filaments branching away from the central structure.

● Bird feathers differ in size and shape all over their bodies. *Sinosauropteryx* feathers ran in tracts along the back, neck, and even the head, creating a downy mohican hairstyle, and were a similar length and shape all over the body.

● Downy feathers help keep birds warm, and were probably used by *Sinosauropteryx* for the same reason. Scientists have suggested *Sinosauropteryx* feathers be named "protofeathers," as they are the forerunners of modern bird feathers.

● Interestingly, there are many theropod dinosaurs, such as *T.rex* and *Velociraptor*, that are more closely related to birds than *Sinosauropteryx*. Perhaps baby *T.rex* were covered in an insulating coat of fluffy feathers!

| 140 | 135 | 130 | 125 | 120 | 115 | 110 | 105 | 100 | 95 | 90 | 85 | 80 | 75 | 70 | 65 MILLION YEARS AGO |

EARLY CRETACEOUS

two legged

Probably the most famous of all dinosaurs, *Tyrannosaurus rex* (*T.rex*)—king of the tyrant lizards—
lived at the end of the Cretaceous period on the huge floodplains of western North America, from
Alberta in Canada down to New Mexico in the United States, just before the dinosaurs died out.

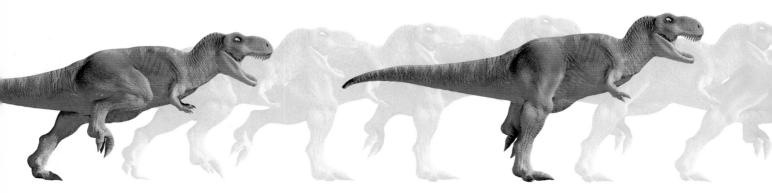

● *T.rex* was a huge, bipedal carnivore over 10ft (3m) tall and weighing six tons. The environment it lived in was dotted with rivers, lakes, and pockets of lush woodland full of ferns, flowering plants, and trees such as conifers, sycamores, and Monkey Puzzles.

● *T.rex* searched these woodland areas for live prey such as *Triceratops* and *Edmontosaurus*. Sometimes it succeeded: a piece of fossilised *T.rex* dung is packed full of semi-digested *Edmontosaurus* bones.

● *T.rex* might have used ambush tactics to catch its prey, bursting out of the trees to catch its startled victim. Forward-facing eyes helped pinpoint prey and also helped *T.rex* avoid dangerous obstacles such as fallen tree trunks and stubby clumps of ferns.

● There is nothing similar to *T.rex* alive today, and this makes locomotion comparisons with modern animals very difficult. Studies have shown that *T.rex* had remarkably long legs.

| 228 | 225 | 220 | 215 | 210 | 205 | 200 | 195 | 190 | 185 | 180 | 175 | 170 | 165 | 160 | 155 | 150 |

● The long bones of the feet are fused together to transfer the huge forces generated by its heavy footfalls through the legs to the rest of the body. These features indicate that *T.rex* had an active way of life.

● There is still disagreement over how fast *T.rex* moved. Estimates range from a leisurely 11mph (18km/h) to a very fast 45mph (72km/h)!

● Those scientists who believe that *T.rex* could move quickly point out that its legs were similar to those of small, fast-running ornithomimids like *Struthiomimus* (pp. 78–79).

● Another study found that *T.rex* did not have enough leg muscle to allow it to run quickly—and it may not have even run at all. This study estimated *T.rex* speed to be between 11–25mph (18–40km/h), slower than an Olympic sprinter.

| 140 | 135 | 130 | 125 | 120 | 115 | 110 | 105 | 100 | 95 | 90 | 85 | 80 | 75 | 70 | 65 | MILLION YEARS AGO |

LATE CRETACEOUS

tyrannosaurus rex 2

On the previous page we were introduced to the disagreement over how fast *T.rex* could move.
Some researchers have used a different approach to investigate *T.rex* speeds, calculating how
badly the animal would be injured if it tripped over.

● Other scientists have noted that as animals increase in size, their legs are held pillar-like beneath the body and bones become thicker to support the extra weight. Heavy, straight-legged animals generally cannot run fast, so perhaps *T.rex* was slow.

● Only one possible *T.rex* footprint has been discovered in New Mexico, and measures nearly 3ft (1m) long. If whole trackways are found, we will have a better idea of how fast *T.rex* could move.

● Even if it could not run, *T.rex*'s long legs helped it move quickly during a fast walk. It is important to remember that to feed and survive, *T.rex* had only to be as fast as its large herbivorous prey, or be able to use ambush techniques, to catch unaware prey.

● Bipedal animals are at a greater risk of falling during bursts of high speed. If a quadruped stumbles, its arms and legs can be positioned to stop it falling over. When a biped trips up, if it cannot bring its legs back underneath its body in time, it falls over.

228	225	220	215	210	205	200	195	190	185	180	175	170	165	160	155	150

● Falls were especially dangerous for *T.rex* because its head had a long way to fall—over 10ft (3m)—and its tiny arms, although strong, could not break its fall. Ostriches have a similar problem, but their heads are small and light, so injuries are less likely.

● If *T.rex* fell over, it risked serious injury and even death. A team of researchers calculated that if a six-ton *T.rex* ran at 45 mph (72km/h) and then tripped, it would hit the ground and skid along at a force that would probably kill it.

● To avoid injury from falls, the researchers calculated that *T.rex* probably kept both feet on the ground for as long as possible during each stride.

● *T.rex* most likely moved at 11–34mph (18–54km/h), similar to the top speed of an African elephant. If *T.rex* fell while moving at this speed, it would be injured and perhaps break some bones, but would probably survive.

| 140 | 135 | 130 | 125 | 120 | 115 | 110 | 105 | 100 | 95 | 90 | 85 | 80 | 75 | 70 | 65 | MILLION YEARS AGO |

LATE CRETACEOUS

struthiomimus

two legged dinosaurs

Struthiomimus (ostrich mimic) was a bipedal dinosaur only 8ft (2.5m) tall and weighing 660lb (300kg), but capable of rapid movement barely matched by the fastest living animals of today. It lived in western Canada in the Late Cretaceous period, around 76 to 70 million years ago.

● With a light but strong skeleton and long, slender legs, *Struthiomimus* was a true cursorial dinosaur. Its elongated leg bones gave it a long stride, and its shinbones (tibia) were much longer than its thigh bones (femur), a feature of birds.

● Muscles attached close to its limb joints ensured that its long legs could move rapidly. The three metatarsal bones of its foot were tightly fused together to effectively transfer footfall forces from its feet through its legs to the rest of its body.

● Coelurosaurs such as *Struthiomimus* were some of the first dinosaurs to arrange their limbs, muscles, and tails in a more bird-like way, with a shorter caudofemoralis leg muscle and a tail that acted more like a rudder for changing direction at high speed.

● With a smaller, lighter tail, *Struthiomimus* would be top-heavy if it did not realign its feet underneath its center of balance. Holding its thigh bone (femur) more horizontally brought its feet forward and rebalanced the animal.

228	225	220	215	210	205	200	195	190	185	180	175	170	165	160	155	150

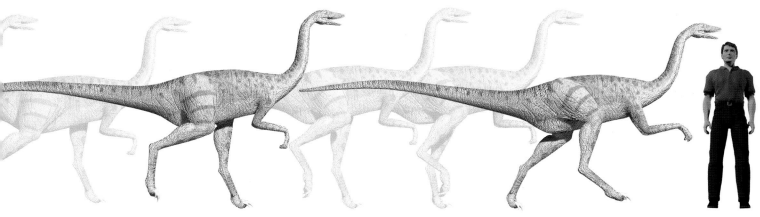

● *Struthiomimus* was very cursorial but did not achieve the supreme cursorial ability seen in modern day ostriches. Well-developed arms and a short but muscular tail meant that *Struthiomimus* was heavier than the flightless, stumpy-tailed ostrich.

● Furthermore, leg bone and muscle arrangements mean that an ostrich can take longer and faster strides than a similar-sized *Struthiomimus*. Ostriches can reach a maximum speed of around 36mph (58km/h).

● Realistic *Struthiomimus* speed estimates range from 22mph (35km/h) to a very fast 31½mph (50km/h). Taking over two strides per second, maximum *Struthiomimus* stride length may have reached 19½ft (6m).

● In addition to escaping from predators, *Struthiomimus* probably used its speed to catch small mammals, lizards, and insects to eat. A long beak, (no teeth), and weak but highly mobile arms suggest it also fed on plants, seeds, and possibly freshwater shellfish.

| 140 | 135 | 130 | 125 | 120 | 115 | 110 | 105 | 100 | 95 | 90 | 85 | 80 | 75 | 70 | 65 | MILLION YEARS AGO |

LATE CRETACEOUS

therizinosaurus

With 27½in (70cm) claws and arms up to 8ft (2.4m) long, *Therizinosaurus* (scythe lizard) appeared

to be a terrifying theropod dinosaur. In fact the opposite was true—it was a waddling herbivore,

with a very unusual-looking skeleton.

● *Therizinosaurus* was a truly bizarre theropod dinosaur. 39ft (12m) long, it was discovered in Mongolia in the early 20th century when scientists uncovered a huge pair of arms tipped with very long claws.

● *Therizinosaurus* was a coelurosaur theropod, with a small head and probably a toothless beak. It had a long, relatively straight neck and a vertebral column that slanted upward from the hips, rather than horizontally as seen in most theropods.

● Some of the hip bones rotated backward to keep the leg and tail muscles working efficiently despite the tilted body. The tail remained horizontal.

● The small but long skull was not suited for eating tough, chewy flesh. *Therizinosaurus* lived in Late Cretaceous wooded riverside forests where it probably used its beak to crop leaves and other plant matter from trees.

| 228 | 225 | 220 | 215 | 210 | 205 | 200 | 195 | 190 | 185 | 180 | 175 | 170 | 165 | 160 | 155 | 150 |

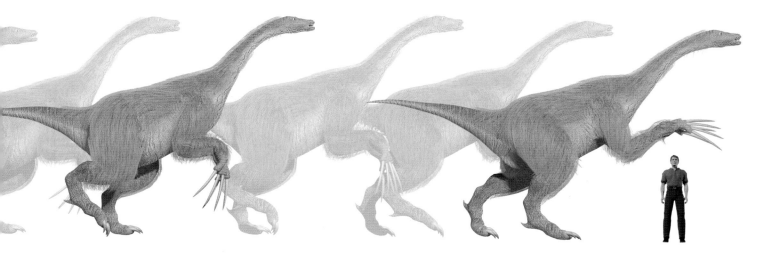

● Further evidence for an herbivorous lifestyle comes from the broad hips. Even though the thigh bone (femur) was angled forward rather than straight down, there was ample space for a large, fermenting gut to be slung between the long legs.

● *Therizinosaurus*'s legs were very powerful, but its broad hips and huge belly gave it a "waddling" gait so it could not run fast, if at all. It lived like a gorilla or an extinct giant ground sloth, moving slowly through the forest, eating at leisure.

● Each claw was longer than your arm and narrow like a large sickle, but was probably too long for attacking or grasping prey. *Therizinosaurus* also had very flexible wrist bones and could tuck its arms into its body in the same way that a bird can fold its wings.

● This flexibility helped *Therizinosaurus* snag greenery, and the claws may have been used to hook twigs or even break open termite mounds.

| 140 | 135 | 130 | 125 | 120 | 115 | 110 | 105 | 100 | 95 | 90 | 85 | 80 | 75 | 70 | 65 MILLION YEARS AGO |

LATE CRETACEOUS

oviraptor

Oviraptor (egg thief) lived around freshwater lakes in the dry Late Cretaceous lands of what is now the Gobi desert in Mongolia. Scientists originally found *Oviraptor* skeletons lying on top of a dinosaur nest and presumed the creature had been fossilized in the act of devouring eggs.

● In fact, recent fossil discoveries have shown that some of the eggs contained *Oviraptor* embryos. So rather than feasting on the contents of the nest, *Oviraptor* was incubating and protecting her brood.

● *Oviraptor* was a theropod dinosaur that grew to around 6½ft (2m) long and weighed up to 130lb (60kg). Its skull was topped with an unusual narrow crest ending in a large toothless beak. It may have fed on freshwater shellfish, other animals, or plants.

● Whatever *Oviraptor* fed on, it was cursorial and fast. Its top speed has been estimated at 24mph (39km/h). Its hindlimbs were long and slender, and its shinbones were about 25 percent longer than the thigh bones.

● *Oviraptor* belongs to a group of "grasping hand" (maniraptor) coelurosaur theropods. Maniraptorans are closely related to birds and have a number of changes to their skeleton that can be seen later in birds.

228	225	220	215	210	205	200	195	190	185	180	175	170	165	160	155	150

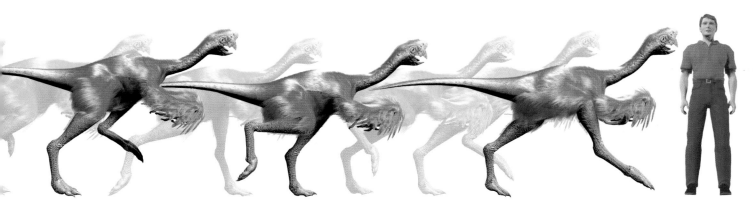

● For example, the tail is short and the hip muscles that move the knees and shins are more important than those that move the thighs. Also, the pelvis is firmly fixed to the vertebral column, and it has a forward-pointing pubic bone and a raised first toe.

● The arms were very long, even though *Oviraptor* did not walk on all fours. Bird-like features can be seen here too. There was a large, U-shaped wishbone and a plate-like sheet of bone in front of the chest called the sternum.

● The arms were able to move in a variety of directions, helped by a half-moon-shaped wrist bone that enabled the hands to be flexed sideways as well as up and down. This is important as the hands were very long and ended in powerful claws.

● *Oviraptor* could fold its hands (like living birds fold their wings) then rotate its arms forward at lightning speed to snatch prey. Hand muscles later became adapted for flapping wings in birds. *Oviraptor* may also have been covered in downy feathers.

| 140 | 135 | 130 | 125 | 120 | 115 | 110 | 105 | 100 | 95 | 90 | 85 | 80 | 75 | 70 | 65 | MILLION YEARS AGO |

LATE CRETACEOUS

caudipteryx

two legged dinosaurs

Caudipteryx (tail feather) lived in Early Cretaceous woodland about 125 to 119 million years ago in what is now north-eastern China. It lived alongside other feathered and fuzz-covered dinosaurs such as *Sinosauropteryx*. It was a turkey-sized dinosaur, about 27½in (70cm) tall and 3ft (1m) long.

● *Caudipteryx* was a remarkable dinosaur. Features of the skull, arms, and hips tell us it was an advanced theropod, yet it possessed a complete covering of feathers, including wing-like arms and an elaborate tail fan.

● *Caudipteryx* had a bird-like beak lined with long teeth along the upper tip. Stones found in its stomach were probably "gastroliths," pieces of rock swallowed by the animal to help grind up food. Creatures that use such stones are usually herbivores.

● *Caudipteryx* had very long legs. It was an extremely cursorial animal and probably a very fast runner, although no one has formally estimated its speed. As it was not running to catch prey, its speed was probably used to quickly evade predators.

● *Caudipteryx* had one of the shortest known dinosaur tails. This affected how the legs were held, as there was little space for the caudofemoralis muscle. As in maniraptoran theropods, the muscles that bent the leg at the knee became very important.

228	225	220	215	210	205	200	195	190	185	180	175	170	165	160	155	150

● Reducing the size of the tail made the body top-heavy. The thigh bone (femur) was probably held quite horizontally, rather than vertically, to help bring the feet forward and balance the body. *Caudipteryx* may have run like an ostrich.

● An ornate fan of feathers, up to 8in (20cm) long, spread out from the short tail bones and acted as stabilizers during fast running. Similar feathers ran along the arms and fingers. These feathers were very close to modern bird feathers.

● Feather shape and overall body plan show that *Caudipteryx* was not a flying animal. The long feathers could have been brightly colored and used for display, to frighten enemies or attract mates.

● The rest of its body was covered in soft, downy feathers. These may have been used to insulate the body against the cold. If *Caudipteryx* was warm-blooded and producing its own body heat, insulation would have been very important.

| 140 | 135 | 130 | 125 | 120 | 115 | 110 | 105 | 100 | 95 | 90 | 85 | 80 | 75 | 70 | 65 | MILLION YEARS AGO |

EARLY CRETACEOUS

Velociraptor (swift robber) stalked Late Cretaceous sand dunes in Mongolia and China between 80 and 73 million years ago. While potential prey such as the small-horned dinosaur *Protoceratops* gathered in herds around watering holes, *Velociraptor* hunted alone or in packs, picking out vulnerable or careless animals.

● *Velociraptor* was a small, aggressive and intelligent dinosaur, 6ft (1.8m) long. It is a member of a group of theropods called dromaeosaurs (running lizards) that have a very large claw on the second toe.

● In *Velociraptor*, this claw was twice as large as its two other toe claws and when covered with a sharp sheath, measured about 3in (8cm) long. The claw was held elevated during normal locomotion, so *Velociraptor* usually walked on only two toes.

● *Velociraptor* had a strange, modified tail. Flattened and elongated bony prongs extended forward and backward from certain tail vertebrae, locking the end two-thirds of the tail into a rigid rod. The base of the tail, near the hips, remained flexible.

● There was little space at the base of the tail to attach the caudofemoralis muscle, which had been reduced in size and effect. Now the tail could move independently of the legs to help balance during running and prey capture.

228	225	220	215	210	205	200	195	190	185	180	175	170	165	160	155	150

● As the heavy tail muscles got smaller, *Velociraptor* probably held its thigh bone (femur) quite horizontally to bring its feet further forward for balance, as the body was top-heavy. The muscles that moved the shins about the knees then developed in a bird-like fashion.

● This was different to the old-style rotation of the thigh bone (femur) around the hip. The pubis bone, which points forward in most theropods, points backward in *Velociraptor*. This is also a more bird-like arrangement.

● *Velociraptor* had very strong shoulders, long arms, and large clawed hands. The leg-kicking muscles and toe-flexing muscles were well-developed and operated the raised claw like a deadly switchblade knife.

● A fossil actually preserves a *Velociraptor* grasping the head of a *Protoceratops* while attempting to slice through its belly with its hind claws. *Protoceratops* has clamped its jaws around *Velociraptor*'s right arm, the two enemies locked in combat.

| 140 | 135 | 130 | 125 | 120 | 115 | 110 | 105 | 100 | 95 | 90 | 85 | 80 | 75 | 70 | 65 | MILLION YEARS AGO |

LATE CRETACEOUS

deinonychus

Deinonychus (terrible claw) lurked in open woodland in western North America around 119 to 97 million years ago. Larger and even more fearful than *Velociraptor*, *Deinonychus* used its strong, agile body to overcome prey, before slicing through flesh with its phenomenal foot claw.

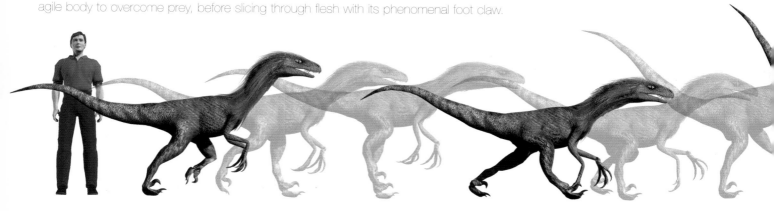

● *Deinonychus* grew up to 11½ft (3.5m) long and probably weighed as much as an adult human. Like *Velociraptor*, it also walked on its third and fourth toes whilst the second toe bore a large sickle-shaped claw, kept off the ground.

● The shape of the toe joints meant the claw could only move up and down, which helped transfer more force to the downward cutting action. The tip of the claw could slice through 150 degrees—nearly half the arc of a circle.

● Most of the tail was held rigid by bony rods, as in *Velociraptor*. The arms and legs were strong and powerful, and shared a number of features with *Velociraptor*. For example, the thigh bone (femur) pointed forward and downward rather than vertically.

● The muscles that moved the shins about the knees were more developed than those that moved the thighs about the hip joint. The shoulders were powerful, and the hands had three fingers tipped with sharp claws. The pubis bone was angled backward.

| 228 | 225 | 220 | 215 | 210 | 205 | 200 | 195 | 190 | 185 | 180 | 175 | 170 | 165 | 160 | 155 | 150 |

● Its long legs produced speeds of up to 19mph (30 km/h). Once prey was in reach, *Deinonychus* launched itself off the ground with arms and legs extended forward, claws ready. While in the air, the tail could act as a rudder to change or maintain direction.

● On impact, powerful jaws clamped around the skin of its prey, backed up by strong arms and shoulders. Toe-flexing muscles brought the claw upward; then special leg muscles contracted, kicking the legs downward in a large circle, slicing its prey.

● *Deinonychus* bones have been found at the same site as the remains of a large herbivorous ornithopod called *Tenontosaurus*. *Tenontosaurus* was unarmored, and young animals would have been obvious targets for *Deinonychus*.

● Large tenontosaurs up to ten times the weight of a single *Deinonychus* appear to have been attacked by packs of six or more predatory animals leaping all over its body in a coordinated assault.

140	135	130	125	120	115	110	105	100	95	90	85	80	75	70	65 MILLION YEARS AGO

MID-CRETACEOUS

archeopteryx
two legged dinosaurs

Archaeopteryx (ancient wing) is probably the most famous fossil of all time as it shows an animal apparently "caught in the act" of evolution. In some ways, *Archaeopteryx* looks like a bird, and in others it resembles a dinosaur. *Archaeopteryx* provides strong support for the idea that birds evolved from theropod dinosaurs.

● *Archaeopteryx* was about the size of a crow. It lived on tropical desert islands about 150 million years ago in what is now southern Germany. Its jaws were lined with small, sharp teeth rather than a beak, and it probably ate insects and other small animals.

● The more advanced theropods could fold their arms like birds were developing bony breastplates, shortening their tails and hips to alter the way they moved, and even had feathers. *Archaeopteryx* had all these features, but is classified as a true bird.

● Its arms and hands were longer than its legs, and were lined with thickly packed feathers. The special position of the main shaft of the feathers tells us these were flight feathers and that *Archaeopteryx* was capable of flapping flight.

● Even so, *Archaeopteryx* was very different to today's birds in having three separate finger bones (instead of a strong fused single rod) and a long tail with feathers along its length (instead of a short and stumpy one with a fan of tail feathers).

228	225	220	215	210	205	200	195	190	185	180	175	170	165	160	155	150

LATE JURASSI

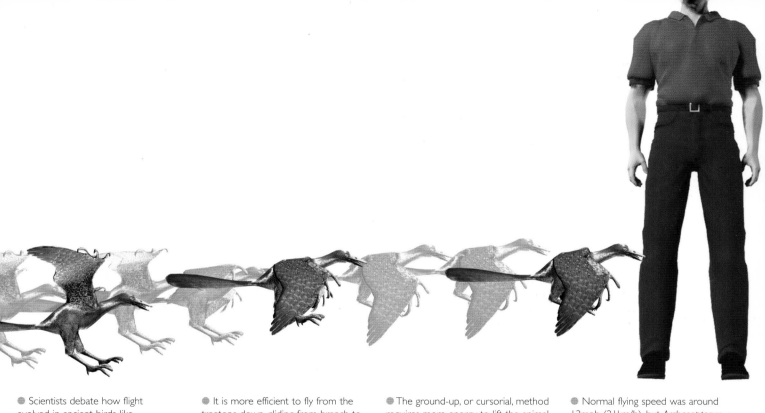

● Scientists debate how flight evolved in ancient birds like *Archaeopteryx*. Some say it learned to fly by gliding down from the treetops; others say that it learned to fly from the ground up.

● It is more efficient to fly from the treetops down, gliding from branch to branch. Flight may have evolved by changing insulation and display feathers into proper flight feathers.

● The ground-up, or cursorial, method requires more energy to lift the animal off the ground than gliding down from the treetops, but since *Archaeopteryx* could run and leap at nearly 18mph (29km/h), it could generate enough lift with its wings to take off.

● Normal flying speed was around 13mph (21km/h), but *Archaeopteryx* was not a skilled flier and could not flap its wings deeply or quickly. It could not control its landings well, and its wishbone didn't store energy like a spring as it does in modern birds.

| 140 | 135 | 130 | 125 | 120 | 115 | 110 | 105 | 100 | 95 | 90 | 85 | 80 | 75 | 70 | 65 MILLION YEARS AGO |

glossary

Apatosaurus: Large, herbivorous sauropod also known as *Brontosaurus*. Lived during the Late Jurassic in the western United States.

Argentinosaurus: Titanosaur sauropod from Argentina. Possibly the largest sauropod that ever lived. Could have weighed up to 100 tons.

Bipedal: An animal that stands and walks on its hind legs only.

Carnivore: An animal that eats only meat. Most theropods were carnivores.

Caudofemoralis: The most powerful leg muscle in most dinosaurs, responsible for pulling the hind legs backward. Ran from the tail to the top of the thigh bone (femur).

Ceratosauria: "Horned lizards." A group of early theropod dinosaurs. All ceratosaurs bore four fingers. Later theropods lost the fourth finger. Includes *Carnotaurus* and *Coelophysis*.

Coelurosaurs: "Hollow-tailed lizards." A group of tetanuran theropods. Includes *Tyrannosaurus rex* and *Velociraptor*.

Cretaceous: The final period of the Mesozoic era, lasting from 144 to 65 million years ago. Dinosaurs became extinct at the end of the Cretaceous period.

Cursorial: An animal with long, slender limbs adapted for fast or long-distance running.

Dew claw: Another name for the first toe (or big toe) of theropod dinosaurs, which is held off the ground. Also known as the "hallux."

Digitigrade: Walking on only the fingers and toes. Dinosaurs and birds are digitigrade. Humans place the whole foot on the ground and are known as plantigrade.

Ectothermic: "Cold-blooded." Ectotherms heat up their bodies using external sources, usually the sun.

Endothermic: "Warm-blooded." Endotherms generate their own constant, internal body heat to keep warm and ensure that bodily processes are working at a high rate.

Extinct: A term used to describe an animal or plant that has died out.

Femur: The single upper bone in the leg; often called the thigh bone.

Fermentation: The breakdown of organic matter (such as plants), often by micro-organisms in the stomach or gut.

Fibula: The smaller of the two lower leg bones that make up the shin. The longer bone is the tibia.

Gait: A specific sequence of leg movements, such as trot, run, or gallop.

Gastroliths: Stones swallowed by some herbivorous dinosaurs and contained within the stomach to help grind up tough food not fully chewed by the teeth.

Genes: Parts of a cell that control features of the body, which are then passed down to the next generation. Eye color is an example.

Graviportal: An animal with thick limb bones arranged as supportive columns beneath the body. Leg muscles are adapted for producing force rather than speed. Means "heavy to carry."

Hadrosaurs: "Bulky lizards." Includes duck-billed dinosaurs like Maiasaura.

Herbivore: An animal that eats only plants. Often has specialized teeth and gut to digest food.

Horsetail: An ancient seedless plant. Common in the Mesozoic, only one type of horsetail survives today.

Humerus: The single upper arm bone.

Ilium: One of the bones of the pelvis (hips). The ilium fuses to special backbone projections called the sacral ribs. The ilium also connects the legs to the rest of the body.

Ischium: One of the bones of the pelvis (hips). It points downward and backward from the hip socket.

Joint: A moveable region in the skeleton where two or more bones meet.

Jurassic: The middle period of the Mesozoic era, lasting from 201 to 144 million years ago. Dinosaurs spread worldwide and birds evolved during this period.

Ligament: Strand, rope, or sheet of soft tissue. Connects bones to each other.

Maniraptors/maniraptorans: A group of coelurosaur, tetanuran theropods with "grasping hands." Includes *Velociraptor* and *Deinonychus*.

Mesozoic: Meaning "middle life." An era of time stretching from approximately 245 to 65 million years ago. Contains the Triassic, Jurassic, and Cretaceous periods.

Metatarsals: The long bones of the foot. Held off the ground during normal walking in dinosaurs. See "digitigrade."

Neovenator: An Early Cretaceous theropod from the Isle of Wight, England.

Omnivore: An animal that eats both plants and meat.

Opposable thumb: When the first digit (thumb) is connected to the palm of the hand at an angle, allowing the whole hand to function as a grasping structure.

Ornithischia: Bird-hipped dinosaurs with a backward-pointing pubis and a predentary bone in the lower jaw. All plant eaters.

Ornithopods: "Bird feet." Plant-eating ornithischian dinosaurs, capable of walking on two or four legs.

Parasagittal: Limbs that are held beneath the body and that only bend forwards and backwards.

Posture: A term used to describe the position of the limbs during standing, walking, or running.

Dinosaurs had an "upright" posture. Lizards have a "sprawling" posture.

Predentary: A small bone found in the lower jaw. Found only in ornithischians where it forms the tip of the beak.

Prosauropods: "Before sauropods." Mainly herbivorous saurischian dinosaurs, capable of walking on either two or four legs. Early relatives of the sauropods.

Pubis: One of the bones of the pelvis (hips). The pubis points downward and backward in most ornithischian dinosaurs and downward and forward in most saurischian dinosaurs.

Quadrupedal: An animal that stands and walks on all fours.

Radius: One of the two bones that make up the lower arm. The other, often larger, bone is the ulna.

Saurischia: Lizard-hipped dinosaurs. Characterised by a forward-facing pubic bone. Theropods, prosauropods, and sauropods are saurischian dinosaurs. One of the two main groups of dinosaurs (see Ornithischians for the other).

Sauropodomorphs: One of the two main groups of saurischian

dinosaurs (the other being theropods). Sauropods and prosauropods are sauropodomorphs.

Sauropods: "Lizard feet." Herbivorous, quadrupedal saurischian dinosaurs. They were the largest of all the dinosaurs with huge bodies, long necks and tails, and pillar-like legs.

Sternum: Equivalent to the breast-bone, a large plate of bone found on the chest to which the ribs attach.

Stride length: The distance covered by the foot during a single step.

Tendon: Sheets or ropes of soft tissue. Arise in muscle and connect muscle to bone.

Tetanuran: "Stiff tails." One of the two major groups of theropod dinosaurs (the other is ceratosaurs). All tetanurans had only three fingers.

Tetrapod: "Four feet." All animals with two arms (or wings) and two legs. Includes animals without limbs that have evolved from four-limbed ancestors, such as snakes.

Theropods: "Beast feet." Mainly predatory saurischian dinosaurs. All were bipedal.

Thyreophorans: "Shield bearers." A group of mainly quadrupedal

herbivorous ornithischian dinosaurs with a bony body-covering. Includes the stegosaurs and ankylosaurs.

Tibia: The larger of the two bones that make up the lower leg or shin. The smaller bone is the fibula.

Titanosaurs: "Gigantic lizards." Large herbivorous sauropods. Included possibly the largest land animal ever, *Argentinosaurus*.

Trackway: A series of footprints made by the same animal.

Triassic: The first period of the Mesozoic era, lasting from 245 to 201 million years ago. Dinosaurs appeared in the middle Triassic.

Ulna: One of the two bones that make up the lower arm. The ulna is often larger than the other bone, the radius.

Vertebra: An individual bone found in the backbone. The backbone is composed of many vertebrae and is also known as the vertebral column.

Wishbone: A bone found in the upper chest of birds and some dinosaurs.

index